Best Wishes
S. Arleaux

Caribbean Cops VI

And Then There Were Twelve

By Stephan M. Arleaux

A Yrag Dualra book

Yrag Dualra Publication, Inc., Jackson Mississippi

CARIBBEAN COPS VI

THIS BOOK CONTAINS THE COMPLETE TEXT OF THE HARDCOVER EDITION.

ISBN-13: 9781495453205

ISBN-10: 1495453200

Other books by Stephan M. Arleaux :

Caribbean Cops , II, III, IV, V, VI, VII, Rex Feral II, III, IV, Murder in Mexico…, Murder In Denver, Murder In Trinidad, Murder in Paradise, Murder By Swap, Cape Arundel Murder, Les Famille Business, The Lady In White, The Lady in black, Angel Of Terror, Moonstone.

These and all past or future publications by this author can be purchased through Amazon.com, and other fine stores by title and author.

This book is for Mary

And the officers of the

VIPD St.Croix

Forward

This novel is an amalgam of truth and fiction. All of the events described are based on actual occurrences, some of which have been slightly altered for the sake of dramatic unity. Some of the characters are a combination of several people; this allows a consolidation for literary efficiency.

Some dates have also been chronologically adjusted. The time is 1991. The Place is Santa Rosa California. As in CC V Rita Troyer ESQ and I, Gary Arlaud PI are still teamed up.

This is a story about a reformed gangster millionaire accused of hireling the murder on another man and the jury who was having a rough time deciding the guilt or innocence of a fellow mortal.

How rough was it? Even Rita and I didn't know for sure.

CHAPTER ONE

It was a few minutes past nine o'clock, five and a half hours after Judge Harrison Cleveland had charged the jury and sent it out lo debate the fate of Vitto 'Falconetti, when the tall, lean-faced jury foreman threw up his hands and cried, "All right, all right, if that's your decision. But do you realize the discomforts involved in being locked up for the night? A second-rate hotel, not even toiletries, probably lumpy beds—"

"Toiletries, schmoiletries," Mrs. Cannon muttered. "It wouldn't be the first time I ever slept in my slip."

"But if we just tried a little longer—"

"Six to six the last three votes, and I'm dead," Mrs. Cannon interrupted again. "I'm really dead. I got this condition."

"Come on, let's give it another hour," Harry Stetler, Juror Number Four, pleaded. "Maybe we can reach a verdict if we talk it over another hour. It's only nine o'clock and I want to get home tonight, if I possibly can. It means a lot to me. Just one more hour."

Louis Kobel, Juror Number Seven shook: his head.

"I want to get home as bad as you do, friend, but let's I face it, we're not going to get together in another hour or, another two hours. Like Mrs. Cannon, I'm lead for sleep. Call the court officer, Robinson,"

Wilton Robinson, the foreman, ran his eyes over the faces of the other eleven, jurors and saw that Kobel was right; three or four of them—Old Man Pepper, Mrs. Cannon, and Mrs. Brown, especially—looked too beat to stay awake another hour. Much less, think straight enough to help reach a verdict. No matter what anybody might think, it was a terribly tiring thing, sitting in the jury box with a man's life at stake, listening to testimony from one side that seemed to prove that Vitto 'Falconetti was a cold-blooded egocentric who had hired a man lo murder his business competitor, and then hearing 'Falconetti's I lawyers tear the testimony apart, and then trying to decide which was true and which was false. No, wonder some; of the jurors looked so rocky. He, Robinson, didn't feel so good himself, headachy, too much cigarette smoke, the awful restaurant food, and the concentration of trying to follow the testimony. Perhaps after a good night's sleep, things would be clearer in everybody's mind. They certainly couldn't be more muddled than they seemed to be

"All right," he said reluctantly. "If that's the way you want it." He waited for somebody to protest, and when Stetler merely shook his head, the foreman went to call the court officer.

Judge Cleveland, who had been reading a mystery I paperback in his chambers, was notified that while the Jury had been unable to reach a verdict, it did not consider itself hopelessly deadlocked. The jurors felt that with a good night's rest, they would be able to reach a unanimous decision, come morning.

The judge dog-eared the page and closed his book. "All right, Mr. Hammersma," he told the court officer. "You'll make the necessary arrangements, thank you." Bring the jury in and I'll give them their instructions. Better, notify Mr. Wolfe and the Troyers, too. I assume they're still here?"

"Yes, sir. The Troyers are with the defendant in the counsel room. The last time I passed by, the guard told me the prisoner was playing gin rummy with Ms. Troyer." Hammersma paused and added, "And winning, too, sir."

"Hm. From what I've seen of 'Falconetti during this trial, he undoubtedly was. He's a—" The judge caught himself and left his chair to walk toward the closet where his judicial robe hung. "You'd better call them in, and Mr. Wolfe, too, Mr. Hanirnersma," he said, almost primly.

But as he flipped into the black robe, Judge Harrison Cleveland thanked his Presbyterian God that a jury would hand down this verdict, not he. For if the law had not required trial by jury for the capital offense and it 'Falconetti had asked to be tried before him, he was damned if he'd with all the testimony in, be able to render a verdict with absolute faith that he was neither condemning a man innocent of this crime nor letting a guilty man walk out free.

Hammersma, the court officer, phoned Wolfe's office and told the Assistant District Attorney that the judge was coming in for lockup instructions. "Does it look hung?" the D.A. asked.

"No, they say they want to sleep on it, that's all." Charley Wolfe was a balding, round-faced man with a snub nose and a potbelly.

Now he rubbed his hand over his face in an unconscious gesture of wearied frustration. He knew he should not ask, that he would get no valid answer, but he had lo have somebody's opinion. "How does it look to you, Ed?" he asked.

He could fairly see the court officer's shrug. "Search me, Mr. Wolfe. You know juries: you get them all figured out one way and they'll step right in the apple pie for you."

"Uh-huh," Wolfe said dismally. 'Thanks. Be right up." The court officer hung up the phone and headed for the counsel room, where Rita Troyer and her PI Gary Arlaud (Arlo). They worked so closely that most referred to them as the Troyers, were closeted with the defendant. It was an unusual arrangement but handy for Hammersma. Ordinarily, the defendant was returned to one of the court's cell-like detention rooms when the jury retired lo deliberate, but some antiquated steam pipes in the ceiling of the hall and detention rooms had burst a couple of days previously, requiring extensive repairs and bringing the judicial decision that all prisoners except maximum-security psychos could be lodged in the counsel rooms, under guard, whenever feasible.

And Vitto 'Falconetti, Hammersma told himself, was no maximum-security psycho, not him. Vitto 'Falconetti had never lost his cool, as the fighters said. Even now, the, court officer would have bet that 'Falconetti was sweating less than the two Troyers. He wondered how the big guy would react lo the knock on the door, even this false alarm; would if be enough to shake him out of that snotty, you-can't-touch-me way of his? The court

9

officer guessed not. About the only thing that would shake up that boy would be 2,000 volts through the seat of the pants— that wasn't the right way to think, especially when, for all Ed Hammersma knew, the guy was innocent. He almost had to be innocent, didn't he, the way he acted in court, like he owned the place and everybody in it.

He reached the counsel room and was greeted by the guard outside the door. "They coming in?" the deputy asked. "What's it going to be, Ed?"

"Yaugh they're comin' in but only for lock-up instructions," the court officer replied. He grimaced before he said, "You and your bets. How do you sleep nights, betting on whether a guy's going to live or die?"

"When the Troyers defend, I always bet them to win. Anything wrong in that?" the guard asked in an injured voice. "I'm on 'Falconetti's side. I'm praying for him."

"And if he loses you hate him for costing you a buck," Hammersma grumbled. He tapped on the door, and when he heard, "Come in," he turned the knob and walked inside.

Rita and Gary pinned their eyes on him, but the prisoner, Vitto 'Falconetti, studied the cards in his hand where he sat at the long counsel table, opposite Gary. 'Falconetti wore the same expression he had carried into court and, before that, into jail, the same attitude he had displayed ever since he had been arrested for complicity in the murder of Daniel Ferriss. One reporter had described this look as "complete unconcern, occasionally touched by something approaching cynical amusement." A handsome man, Vitto: 'Falconetti, in a tough, cold, indrawn way. The eyes that studied the cards (and read them for their value, too, as he remembered Gary's discards) were cat's-eye gray-green and totally expression less. His thick, sandy hair was sprinkled with gray, as were the heavy brows over the clear, carbolic eyes. His nose had been dented during his fantastic career, but the break added to, rather than detracted from, the whole picture; it went: with the rock-hard jaw line, the wide, mocking mouth, the thick neck and wide shoulders, the great frame that relaxed easily at this time, which could well be his moment of truth.

Rita broke the brief silence. "Is the jury coming in Ed?"

"Uh-huh, but no verdict yet, Ms. Troyer. " the court officer replied with a nod. "Judge Cleveland's going to lock 'em up for the night."

"Down for three," Vitto 'Falconetti said. "I've got you by the short hair. Rita.. with your two queens and that jack of diamonds." He spread his cards and gave a short laugh, looked at Rita. "So we have to wait till morning for the yes or no, is that it, Counselor?"

"It looks that way," Rita said. "And is that a good sign or bad?"

Gary gave a faint shake of his bead. "I gave up trying to interpret such things some time ago. Let's hope it's a good sign."

'Falconetti narrowed his eyes a shade. "You sound as though you really mean that," he said, after a pause.

"I'm your attorney; Gary and I worked hard on your defense, so why shouldn't I mean it?"

A shrug of the massive shoulders, "I may be wrong," 'Falconetti said easily, "but I somehow got the idea that it wouldn't break you all up if the jury brought in a guilty verdict—especially since I refused to play it your way and get up on that witness stand."

Rita's month quirked at one comer, "Just so you remember that we did advise you to take the stand, Mr. 'Falconetti," she said cryptically, then added in a brisker tone, "Well, shall we go out and bid the jury "Good night, pleasant dreams, and a whisper of reason. sometime during the night that will change all the guilty ballots to not guilty?"

'Falconetti grinned, unaffectedly but without the slightest warmth. "Looks as though my chances for a ripe old age depend on how well those jurors cork off, eh? And ,you owe me three-sixty-one plus what's in you hand now. How many did I catch you with?"

Gary Arlaud looked at his cards and said, "Thirty-two minus tierce,, twenty-nine. I owe you three-ninety."

"Check," 'Falconetti said pleasantly. "Take it off, your bill if I turn out to be a loser. If I win, we'll flip double or nothing. Okay?"

"Come on." Rita said irritably. "Judge Cleveland is nobody to be kept waiting at any time, much less at this hour."

'Falconetti lounged out of his chair, and as he approached the door he thrust out his thick wrists to take the handcuffs the guard slipped on for the brief trip to the courtroom. The little party moved down the corridor, paused outside the courtroom for the manacles to be removed, and went inside to hear Judge Cleveland give solemn, straight-faced warning to the eight men and four women of the jury that they would not, must not, discuss this trial among themselves until they returned to the jury room in the morning.

Better, tell them they mustn't blink or breathe, Rita Troyer said silently. I wonder if any judges ever believed six pairs of roommates restrained themselves from mentioning the one subject they had in common, the trial that put them where they were. The jurors all nodded with equal solemnity. The judge left the bench, his robe whispering, and the jurors filed out of the courtroom, bound for a hotel a few blocks away. The deputy in charge of Vitto 'Falconetti approached the defense table and put a hand on his prisoner's arm.

The big man gave his cold smile to Rita and Gary and asked, almost jauntily, "See you in the morning, I trust? Don't forget to phone Lou, will you?" He took the Troyer's silent nods with a widening of his mirthless smile and went off with his escort. Rita watched him go, gave a half-shake of her head, and turned back to Gary.

"I suddenly find I'm ravenous," she said. "How about you?" Before her long suffering PI could speak, she added, "Don't say it; I can tell by your expression that you're not. What's happened to your generation that you're satisfied with a snack here and a bite there? You never want a full-course dinner, served with elegance. Too time-consuming, too ritualistic, the same thing's wrong with your literature, completely, hurried, a snack here and a bite there, never the full, relaxed, complete realization."

"When you're through with your diatribe, you might let me see about calling Mrs. 'Falconetti and then getting a cab to Morgan's," Gary said. "They close at ten, you know."

"What are we waiting for?" his Boss asked, and headed for the side door that opened onto the corridor, bound for his overcoat and hat in the counsel room.

"Rita?" Charley Wolfe called from his table. "Got a minute?"

Rita checked her dash and turned back, trying to hide her impatience. "Yes, Charley?"

The Assistant D.A. came across the courtroom toward her, his attaché case in his hand, as Gary kept on going, headed for a phone. Rita had the fleeting thought that Charley looked more tired than even the late hour, and his considerable efforts, in this trial should have made him. Ordinarily, Charley was a fairly ebullient person, sustained by a sincere sense of public service that kept him in the District Attorney's office when be doubtless could have made more money in private practice, but tonight he seemed discouraged, weighed down by problems and frustrations that added ten years to his age.

He must have hoped for a quick verdict, Rita told. herself. He had a right to, I guess. With the main testimony a series of flat contradictions, a jury could be expected to jump one way or the other in the first few minutes of deliberation. If a jury could reasonably, he expected to do a certain thing, given a certain situation. Which it can't.

Wolfe reached her and put on a tired smile. "Another one of those, eh, Rita?" he asked.

"Another one of those," Troyer said, nodding. "Twelve more hours for us to spend wondering why they need more time to return a not-guilty verdict."

"Not guilty! You're surely not expecting—" Wolfe. broke off and hunched his shoulders, too beat to carry on the byplay, voice the assurances of an eventual guilty verdict that would be no more valid than Troyer's prediction of the opposite result. The D.A. hesitated and then asked, "Do you know the percentage of locked-up juries that wind up hung, Rita?"

"I never ran up any figures on it, no. Why do you ask?"

"I've looked over the court records, and it would surprise you. I did it mostly out of curiosity. Maybe III write a paper on it someday—'A Treatise on All-Night Jury Sessions, or. No Verdict, No Bed and Breakfast.'"

Rita laughed dutifully at this delay, which kept her from her filet mignon, medium rare; with rice milanese on the side, a Caesar salad, and before anything else, a dozen Chincoteagues on the half shell.

"Well, they say a slow Jury is a conscientious jury, Charley," she offered. "Maybe we ought to get some consolation out of that. These instant-verdict juries are what worry me more than the locked-up variety. I sometimes get the feeling that they had their minds made up before we chose them."

"Yeah," Wolfe said absently. He looked up at the vacant bench, then at the side door through which 'Falconetti had been taken by his guard, and finally back at Troyer. "Tell me, Rita," he asked, "doesn't the prospect of a hung jury and having to go through this all over again give you the willies?"

Rita hesitated. Charley Wolfe was a good man, a good D.A. with irreproachable ethics; he was not one to try any cute extracurricular trickery with an encounter such as this. Whatever was said now was between the two of them, old friends from 'way back.

"To tell you the truth," Troyer said finally, "the idea fills me with repugnance approaching horror. You saw that I didn't get much pleasure out of this trial, didn't you? Otherwise, you wouldn't have asked that question. Maybe you know me too well."

"I could tell that you and your client weren't in complete rapport," Wolfe said with a nod, "but why I asked you—Rita, I feel the same way you do about another trial. If you want to give it some thought, if that jury deadlocks—well, maybe my office would go along on a ....plea to murder-second." When he saw Rita's expression he added hastily, "I'm not making any promises, but I've sort of sounded out the First Soldier and he wasn't altogether averse to the idea. And I'm pretty sure Judge Cleveland wouldn't present any difficulties."

"How about manslaughter?" Troyer asked.

Wolfe shook his head. "I don't think so but—well, maybe that's not impossible, either. If you want to go into it further, get in touch, at home or the office early tomorrow, before court. It's just possible 'Falconetti might want to—well, he might have a new view on a plea after a night of wondering what that locked-up jury will decide."

Rita pursed her lips. "We'll see, Charley," she said. "I have my doubts that 'Falconetti—well, we'll see. And thanks."

"You're welcome. Good night, Rita."

"Night, Charley. If the jury had been able to finish this up tonight. I'd ask you to have a late supper with Gary and me, but - . ."

"I'm too bushed to eat, anyway. It's home and bed for me." Wolfe turned back to his table across the room, and Troyer hurried down the corridor to the counsel room. As her heels sounded resoundingly on the terrazzo floor, the lawyer said silently, were in 'Falconetti's position—and pray God

I never am—I think I'd jump at a chance to plead to manslaughter or even murder-second. But I'm betting he won't. No, not our boy, Vitto 'Falconetti.

And added immediately, self-reprovingly. But you wouldn't agree to any deal at all if you were innocent, Rita Troyer, and for all you know, Vitto 'Falconetti realty isn't guilty.

****

After leaving the courtroom, the jury in whose hands had been placed the life of Vitto 'Falconetti was marched two by two down a cold, empty street that flanked Administration Square (dark and silent now, the temple of justice brooding over the out-of-step, white-breathed little band) to the Hotel Inness and put to bed.

To put it bluntly, the Inness had seen better days. It had never ranked with the plus ultra, not even when new, but it had been a solid, respectable address widely patronized by legal visitors who, having to come to Santa Rosa on a case, had brought their families along for shopping, sight-seeing in Wine Country, and taking in a couple of shows in San Francisco , just 40 minutes away. It was still respectable enough (a little too dank for assignations, no matter how far off the beaten track), but it missed being a flea bag by a hair. When they were trooped through the archaic lobby, all the jurors' who were not too tired to look about them groaned, some audibly, and most of them wished they had stuck it out for that one more hour that Harry Stetler and the foreman, Walton Robinson, had pleaded for.

"Second floor," said the leading officer, Emerson Welsh, as the jurors paused inside the revolving door. "Might as well use the stairs. The elevator takes forever." Wherewith he led them to the wide staircase that curved up to the shadowy mezzanine.

16

"Me, I'll wait for the elevator," sighed Mrs. Lorraine Brown, Juror Number Five, edging toward one of the deep leather lobby chairs. "My feet are so swollen. I'd never make it to the mezz."

"I'm not supposed to climb stairs," Mrs. Vida Cannoet, Juror Number Ten, complained. "I got this condition."

"Sorry," the officer said again. His voice hid his sympathy well: he had been dealing with jurors for many years and had long since relegated them to three main classes, crabs, kooks, and numbskulls.

"You have to stay together. It's the law."

"Who made such a law?" Mrs., Cannon groaned. "Did I ever vote for such a law? I'll wait for the elevator with Mrs. Brown. We won't say a word; we'll just sit."

"Come on, Mrs. Cannon," the foreman, Robinson, said. "Here, give me your arm; I'll help you. You wouldn't want something to happen that would make this a mistrial and have all our work go out the window for nothing, would you?"

"God forbid!" Mrs. Cannon cried.

"Never mind your arm. I can make it. Rather than sit through that trial for nothing, I'd slide up the banister, could such a thing be done. Listen to that Mr. Wolfe and those Troyers for another million hours, with that man, 'Falconetti, sitting there and—"

"Hey!"

" Both officers barked the word, and Mrs. Cannon jumped as though prodded in a Sensitive spot.

"No talking about the trial, remember," Welsh said.

"The judge told you all about that."

In injured silence Mrs. Cannon permitted herself to be escorted up the stairs. So did Mrs. Brown, complaining bitterly about her swollen feet and why couldn't the people who had charge of these things have gotten them reservations at a nicer place, say the Ramada or anyway the Hilton?

Sixty-four stair steps brought the jurors to the second floor, where Welsh and Kiemey gave out the billeting assignments. Foreman. Robinson and Juror Number Two, George Oliver, took Room 222. Jurors Three and Four, Old Man Pepper and Harry Stetler, were lodged in Room 224. Mrs. Brown and Elsie Harding, Jurors Five and Six, were given Room 226 and into 228 went Jurors Seven and Eight, Louis Kobel and John Gier Jurors Nine and Ten were the other two women of the jury, Ann Alspach (who had been labeled a dish on sight by George Oliver and who had lost none of her allure for George during the grinding hours of the trial) and Mrs. Cannon (who was distinctly not a dish in George's book), and they were assigned to Room 230. The last two jurors Eleven and Twelve, Charles Williams and Anson Benedict, took Room 232, so that when all the 'Falconetti-jury members were finally quartered, they occupied six adjoining rooms on the same side of the corridor.

"Now, you're not supposed to do any visiting between rooms or anything like that," Welsh, explained. "Don't try to make any phone calls, because they have orders downstairs not to clear any outgoing calls through the switchboard or incoming calls, either, in case anybody should try to get in touch with you."

"In this place?" somebody asked bleakly. "We could be in Outer Mongolia."

"If any of you ladies or gentlemen want to notify anybody that you won't be home tonight," the officer went on, "we can get a message to them, tell them not to worry and so forth. Chances are, they read the early morning papers that'll be out in a few minutes or watch TV."

They'll know, anyway; it'll be on the eleven-o'clock news, sure."

"I always wanted to be on television," George Oliver said.

"I figure I can do as well as some of those guys that are getting a million bucks a show. How sweet it is'"

"Come on, come on," Walton Robinson said irritably "let's cut out the clowning and get some sleep. Anybody want to send a message to anybody, tell them they're all right?"

"You call this all right?" Harold Stetier grumbled.

It turned out that five jurors wanted to send messages, Mrs. Cannon and Mrs. Brown (of course), Old Man Pepper, Kobel, and Williams. Apparently, neither of the two younger women jurors, the dish, Ann Alspach, and Elsie Harding, had anyone who might pace the floor in their absence. This gave Oliver more reason to believe that the wedding ring Ann wore was no barrier to further pursuit once this trial was over; he figured she was either a young widow or that if there was a Mr. Alspach, he didn't count much, not by the looks she had given him almost from the word go.

"Okay, then," Welsh said when he had written down names and phone numbers for the five Jurors, "everybody in their rooms and no socializing, remember, no talking over the case, like the judge said. Good night, everybody, and sweet dreams."

****

In his cell, Vitto 'Falconetti lay on his cot, smoking a cigarette and looking up at the bare ceiling and wondering whether the jury, those eight jerky knot-heads, the two old bags, and the two young broads, were going to vote yes or no.

Or maybe, he cautioned himself, he should think of those jurors in more respectful terms. Maybe there was something to Kicky Dimne's old theory that if you thought bad thoughts about a guy while he was asleep, these contemptuous or treacherous thoughts somehow seeped into the sleeping guy's brain, and when he woke up the next morning he had you pegged for a wrong guy; he might not know why, but you would never again be able to con him into thinking you were his friend.

"During the day you can think anything you want to about the guy," Kicky used to counsel, seriously, "and he'll never know it—he'll be too busy walkin' around and talkin' and scramblin' for the buck. But at night, if you want to keep him thinkin' you're on his side while you're gettin' ready to ream him, don't think nothin' but nice things about the bastard. And try to think like you really meant it."

'Falconetti smiled in the semidarkness. E.S.P., Hell's Kitchen variety. Good old Kicky, the nut. He had been full of such pearls of wisdom, and some of them, at least, must have been valid because he played all the angles, crossed many a dangerous man in his day, and yet must have been pushing forty before everything caught up with him and they found him behind a billboard, full of holes probably made with an ice pick.

Billboard. The body of Dan Ferriss had also been found behind a billboard, but in another part of the country from where Kicky's punctured corpse had been discovered. Handsome Dan had been found in a vacant lot at the comer of Houston and Mulberry, and he hadn't been ice picked; the back of his head had been blown out by a .45 slug. Or at least that was what the cops had said. That was what they'd testified on the witness stand, sitting there in their schlock civilian suits with the badge over the breast pocket, reciting the facts in that prim, unnatural way they'd been taught to speak in court. Once a with that someone had been one Herbert Jaffee, who had been hired by the defendant in this case, Vitto 'Falconetti, to kill Dan Ferriss for the sum of $10,000. Motive: 'Falconetti's determination to erase the one competitor who threatened his domination of the brickwork industry on the west coast and its immediate environs.

'Falconetti dragged at his cigarette, then dangled his long arm over the side of his bunk, reaching for the coffee tin that served him for an ashtray. He stubbed out his smoke, clasped his hands behind his head, and continued his study of the dark cell ceiling.

Ordinarily, he considered time spent dwelling on memories or indulging in introspection as time wasted, but now he lei his thoughts wander off the

20

leash. So what if they turned up some things he'd rather forget. So he could take them all, good or bad, and put them right back where they belonged after he'd looked them over, just for kicks, something to do.

Let them go way back to the day when he wasn't Vitto 'Falconetti at all, to the time when he was a tough little hoodlum with a name a block long, as mean as one of the rats that infested the slum tenement where he was born. Never mind the real name; there might be a thousand cousins and such who would try to get in his hair the minute the real name was known. ("Look, look, we got a millionaire- in the family, let's put the sleeve on him good.") He didn't wear the name long, anyway; even when he was still living at "home," dodging his mother's invective and thrown crockery and his crazy-drunk father's more dangerous hooked hands, he used the name 'Falconetti on the streets. Funny, he had forgotten just why he had picked the name Vitto 'Falconetti. Possibly he had admired the athlete, Jim 'Falconetti, but he doubted it—who ever heard of Jim 'Falconetti or any other football star in Hell's Kitchen in those days? The Jints, yes, Hans Lobert, Benny Kauff, Heiflie Groh, Fred Snodgrass, and the others, but football was something the college boys played.

Anyway, he was Franky 'Falconetti when he was taken into Little Red O'Neil's gang, at the age of twelve. Most of the gangs had names but not O'Neil's; Little Red hadn't had to put a fancy tag on his boys to let everybody know that his was a hard crowd. In all Hell's Kitchen they were the toughest. They lived by burglary, lush rolling, holdup, and occasional murder, and they lived higher than their parents had ever been able to manage, maintaining "club rooms" in a rented basement that they furnished by thievery and staffed with girls as hard as they, or harder, to do the cooking, tend to their sexual needs, and occasionally to hit the streets to bring in some money or more often to deliver a staked-out high roller from uptown into their hands.

Vitto's girl was Milly, whom he had inherited when her original boyfriend, Ossie Vinceletta, had disappeared, presumed dead. Milly was five or six years older than Vitto, but he was big for his age so they did not look mismatched. It was from Milly that Vitto learned the facts of life, or

21

rather, since he had known all about everything from the time he had been able to look and listen, she taught him the practical application of these aforesaid facts.

It was possibly due to Millie's older, wiser head that. Vitto moved up in the gang so rapidly, from spotter to lockout to participating member of a loft-worker crew. When Little Red O'Neil hired his gang out to a New Jersey mobster who was trying to crack the jealously guarded Manhattan Belgian alcohol market, Vitto 'Falconetti progressed to the position of pineapple man and hemstitcher. He never knew how many people he killed with his bombs and submachine-gun fire, but it must have been a considerable number because his operations were chiefly responsible for bringing down on Little Red's gang the combined wrath of the established mob lords. One evening when 'Falconetti was cheating on Milly in a fifty-dollar house some thirty blocks away, O'Neil's "clubhouse" was fire-bombed and those who tried to escape the flames were shot gunned down.   That was the end not only of the gang but also of Vitto 'Falconetti's promising career as a hoodlum, as well. He was lucky enough to be loaded with dough when his companions and his livelihood were wiped out, and he was doubly fortunate to be graced with a startling conviction, come out of nowhere. Although he knew he would have no trouble hiring out his talents to some other gang, he also found himself knowing just as surely that if he did he would wind up as Little Red, Milly, and the others had, within a few years, months, weeks, or even days.

He was never able to account for what he did next. He moved to that strange, mysterious territory known as San Francisco California, and there he entered a trade school to learn how to be a bricklayer. He did not change his assumed name or make any other effort to disguise his identity; for some reason it never entered his mind that the same forces that had so cruelly erased Little Red and his gang would still want to do him any harm. His innocent faith that what was over, was over, and proved out: he was a living refutation of the axiom that once a man enters the rackets he will never leave them alive

For 'Falconetti not only lived, he prospered beyond the wildest happy endings ever conceived by the late Horatio Alger. Now, at fifty-five, he was a millionaire with a beautiful wife, a duplex apartment, in the best part of town, a couple to take care of the apartment, a chauffeur-driven Bentley for Louise, a nice little custom-built Alfa Romeo for himself, and a walk-in closet full of expensive suits, shoes, and other gent's furnishings.

He was also lying on a prison cot, charged with complicity in the murder of Daniel M. Ferriss, and a reminder of this fact was the approaching footsteps that echoed in tile corridor outside.

'Falconetti muttered a curse under his breath. He could take—had taken—about everything they had dealt him without giving the sonsabitches the satisfaction of seeing anything on his face about how lie felt, but if Stanley ..McGuirk bugged him just one more time he was liable to break out in the screaming sweats. Stanley McGuirk was the night guard on this cellblock—the turnkey, 'Falconetti supposed he was called—and Stanley was a talker. He had the skin of a rhinoceros, the humor of a sick buzzard, and the unquenchable conviction that his duty in life was to cheer the lot of his prisoners with his chatter.

'Falconetti considered feigning sleep but decided against it: Stanley would only cough or bang the bars "accidentally" to wake him up, and some of the other boys in the cellblock would be wakened, too. Not that Vitto gave a damn about any of those poor slobs losing sleep on his account, but when McGuirk finished with him he would probably engage another of the wakeful in his idea of consoling conversation, and this could keep up until he went off duty.

So 'Falconetti lit another cigarette as- the guard, short, skinny (How did he ever get through the Police Academy, anyway, or do ward bosses get turnkeys their jobs?), reached the front of his cell and peered in.

"You awake?" he asked. He had a peculiarly irritating tone of voice, a whine with an undercoating of authority, the voice of a nothing with a badge—or a ring of keys.

'Falconetti did not answer. Instead, he blew cigarette smoke at the ceiling.

"I don't blame you," McGuirk said. "I wouldn't be sleeping, neither, if you know what I mean." 'Falconetti took another puff and exhaled again.

"You. figure they could go out and argue a little bit and then decide," the guard kept on. "What do they need overnight for? If you know what I mean."

The man on the cot grunted, swung his legs over the side, and sat up, cradling his cigarette in his cupped hand, looking down. at the curling smoke, trying to command his jumping nerves to be still.

"I mean, how thorough can you get?" McGuirk asked. His authoritative whine took on a buzz-saw edge as he explained his own erudition. "I mean, you can go over the facts just so much." He gave a whinnying laugh. "Boy, any shrimp can be a juror. My old lady was a juror last year." He laughed again. "Jesus, I'd hate to be on trial when she's sittin' up there in the jury box, that's for sure. She'd string up her own son, which happens to be me."

At this unseemly hour of eleven fifteen, one and a quarter hours after the doors of Aliotos's had been firmly closed and curtained, henceforth to open only to speed departing guests on their way. There at Thirty-seven sat Rita Troyer and Gary Arlaud, and, While Gary was aware of the reproachful glances of Frederick, the maitre d', and the downright hatred in the glare of their table waiter, Rita seemed oblivious to both, as she ate and ate and ate

Gary had seen his Boss in the grip of one of these compulsive eating Jags on a few previous occasions and always under the same conditions. While other men might seek the jug for relief from tension and inner doubts that had built up under stress like that which Rita Troyer had undergone during the past several days, Rita took recourse to prodigious eating or exercise on the squash court that left her physically exhausted. Usually it was the squash court, but as the hour of the 'Falconetti jury's lockup had been too late for this, Rita Troyer had to eat and Frederick and the waiter, poor fellows, would have to bear with her.

They had made the restaurant just under the wire, following the last-minute delay caused by the conference with Wolfe. Frederick had been just about to snap the night latch and pull shut the shade when the Troyers' cab had disgorged them at the curb, and Gary had known by the headwaiter's expression that if both had not been such good tippers, such congenial guests on so many occasions, and if Rita had not helped Frederick's nephew's against a charge of impairing the morals of a minor that had turned out to be a case of mistaken identify, the word would have been, "So sorry, but we're closing."

But now, seventy-five minutes later, Gary also knew that they had overstayed their welcome, even as big tippers, good regular customers, and defenders of innocent nephews. Unless some other of Frederick's kin ran afoul of the law in the near future and needed counsel, the two Troyers (as Rita and Gary were known together)could expect to be seated next to the kitchen door the next time either of them came into Aliotos and after that they would have to work their way toward the better tables with tips that made no sense at all.

Gary sighed. He freely admitted that he might well be the first of the big-time tightwads, at least at heart, but it galled him to have to pay twenty per cent of the bill, and up, to escape insult and possibly ptomaine in a restaurant whose carte listed half a grapefruit at $6.25. He never had seen the justice in having to give a surly, unshaven, un bathed cab driver a half-dollar tip for a dollar haul without getting so much as a thank-you in return, and as for hotel doormen . . .

"I know they make their living on tips," he had complained to his boss on occasion, "but why should they have to? Why not—?"

"A thing of custom; 'tis no other; only it spoils the pleasure of the time," Rita had quoted, breaking in. "Seriously, though, have you ever eaten in a restaurant where fifteen per cent was automatically added to the bill and no tips were required?" "No, they tried it at the club but—"

"But they found out it didn't work. All it produced was terrible service, lackadaisically applied."

"But they add the automatic tip abroad and it works," Gary had protested.

"Abroad is not here," Rita had explained. "American free enterprise needs incentive. It's our great system and no better can be found on the face of the earth and we're stuck with tipping, a means of incentive." And had added after a pause, "And of course agree with you about coercive tipping, but who am I to join a crusade when it brings only indigestion and a cold in the head from a drafty table, cunningly placed by the management to take care of stiffs?"

But now, Gary thought gloomily, no tip was going to be big enough to calm the hatred of their table waiter. From the black looks he cast them, by the way he constantly refilled their water glasses and flapped his napkin at the few uncluttered spots on their table, this was obviously the night the waiter was going to make out with a goddess he had been trying to get next to for several years.

"We'll be going in a second," he said humbly as the waiter approached yet another lime. "The check, please."

"Hold on," Rita protested. "I haven't even begun to think about dessert yet." He looked blandly up at the waiter's returning scowl. "What do you suggest for dessert, something not too Light?"

"I'm sorry, Madam," the dark-faced man said in a stilted voice, "but the kitchen is closed. I'm afraid there is no dessert."

"Oh, there must be something in the refrigerator," Troyer said with impenetrable geniality. "Go take a look, will you, please?"

The waiter half-hesitated, then hurried off, muttering under his breath. Gary looked after him and then back at his Boss. "I'd hate to eat what he

26

finds, if he finds anything. Which I'll bet you twenty to one he won't. Fifty to one."

"Bad syntax," Rita said. "Are you going to finish that whatever-it-is?"

"It's zucchini and it's stone cold and no, I'm not going to finish it.

"Pass it over, then. I'm still hungry." Gary handed over the side dish, his nose wrinkled. "What happened to your diet?" he asked as Rita plunged into the zucchini.

"I gave it up," his Boss retorted tersely.

"You just started it this morning."

Rita laughed." Pass the bread,"

"Honestly, you've got about as much will power as a flounder."

Rita swallowed and said, "If there was a flounder on the table, I'd eat that, too." She flourished her fork. "'Eat, drink, and be merry; this is a celebration.!"

Gary frowned. "A celebration before the verdict's in?"

"Right. I'm celebrating the fact that I got through this case without losing my temper or shading one little ethical principle in defending our unwholesome client. That calls for a celebration, doesn't it? I've never been so, glad to be finished with a case in my whole long, gaudy career. May I have the butter please?"

"Well, I wouldn't call this case my keenest delight myself," he agreed, "but I hope we win. The thing that bothers me a little is my reasons for hoping that."

He waited while Rita bolted more bread and butter, then a forkful of the zucchini he had found so tasteless.

"Don't let your reasons bother you," Rita said finally. "We're supposed to win, you know." She forked up another mouthful. "I feel so good I even like this zucchini, which I hate."

"For the love of mike, let's get out of here," Gary said as his Leader chewed on. "We can stop at a Nedick's on the way to my place if you feel faint from hunger."

"We're paying for this, we're eating this," Rita argued. "Too many times have I gotten Up from a table here in Aliotos with twenty dollars worth of food lying on my plate, untouched. This is just my way of balancing things out."

"I'm very sorry, sir," the waiter said from behind Gary, his voice completely hiding any trace of regret, "but there is no dessert. Did you say something about the check?"

"I'll take it," Gary said hastily, before his boss could move for re-argument on the no-dessert ruling. He took the square cardboard from the salver that the waiter whipped from behind his back, glanced at it long enough to wince, and then scribbled his name, lurched in his chair to get his wallet out of his hip pocket, and put a bill of insanely large denomination on the face-down check.

"Thanks," the waiter said, and departed, his hatred unassuaged.

"Ready?" Gary asked blightly but without much hope.

"No," said Rita flatly. "I'll not be rushed. You were speaking of being bothered by reasons. Elucidate. Be brisk as a bee in conversation, like Tom Birch."

"Who," Gary asked heavily, "is or was Tom Birch?"

"Pal of Dr. Johnson, according to Bosweil. Brisk as a bee in conversation, but the minute he picked up a pen his mind went blank. Or so Bosweil said know, this zucchini isn't bad at all. What about your botherment over your reasons?"

Gary sighed and lit a cigarette. "Well, sometimes it's like I'm working for my own ego instead of working for our client."

"Or you feel you may be working for some philosophical concept of justice instead of for the man," Rita said, nodding. "I know what you mean. It's a self-doubt that's been raising its ugly head for centuries, I imagine."

She forked up the last of the zucchini, chewed and swallowed. "The result's the same, Gary," he went on. "We win every once in a while we're bound to want to win a case just for us because we need reassurance that were good lawyers."

"It sounds selfish, somehow," Gary murmured.

"Not selfish, only human," his boss corrected. "And that's how I felt about this case. Vitto 'Falconetti is an evil and violent man, and society would probably be better off if he was put away. But if that jury frees him, I'll be proud of our work and sorry that he's still walking around."

"Do you think he's guilty, then?" Gary asked.

Rita shrugged, "I plead ignorance We did our job. We protected his civil liberties, and that's more important than anything else."

Gary looked down at his cigarette and scowled. "I despise that man," he said slowly.

"So do I," Rita agreed. "And now, if you're through lollygagging at table, how about getting out of here? We've held these poor hard-working people here far too long, as it is. Damned shame."

CHAPTER TWO

At the Hotel Inness, Officer Emerson Welsh yawned, stretched, and consulted his wristwatch. Not trusting its message and needing to get up and walk around before he became completely butt-sprung, anyway, he left his chair at one end of the passageway and walked to the other where sat Jim Kiemey, reading a paperback that, from the looks of his face, must have been hot stuff. "What time you got, Jim?" Welsh demanded.

Kiemey reluctantly tore his fascinated gaze from the printed page and looked at his watch. "Twenty past eleven."

Welsh frowned at his watch and said, "I got twenty two past. This thing is driving me out of my skull. It gains two minutes a day, regular as clockwork." Kierney laughed. "What's two minutes a day to a man like you, a man whose life is dedicated to sitting in halls to make sure jurors don't talk to each other when they're not supposed to?"

"Yeah," the other guard grumped. "Some job, huh? They can put it on my tombstone, he sprained his tail sittin' guard on dumb jurors. They hit the sack and conked off the minute we shut'em in. Or if they're talkin', how are we supposed to stop'em, I mean the two in each room? Maybe we ought to listen at the keyhole or peek.

"As far as that goes," Kiemey said, "I wouldn't mind lookin' over the transom at that one babe, the one in Two-Thirty a bit. Boy, what a body. What I could do with some of that."

Welsh yawned again and knuckled his head just over his ear. "Yeah, you'd raise hell, you would," he jeered. "Lookin' over the transom would be about as far as you could go. That and readin' books about it."

"This?" Kiemey asked, affronted. He turned the cover of his paperback toward his partner. "This is no Fanny Hill, like the last one. This is brainy stuff. Educational. All about the olden times, like before the Civil War."

"I bet." Welsh stretched again. "I'm goin' for a sandwich and a cup of coffee. Mind the store, will you?"

"Uh-huh, but don't take all night. I could do with something to eat myself." "You want I should bring you something?"

"No, I'll go out when you come back. So don't get into any political arguments, will you?"

"Be right back," Welsh lied. He started down the hall, glanced at the door of Room 222, and then looked back at his partner. "Y'know, I half-think they enjoy bein' locked up for the night like this."

"In this crummy hotel?" Kiemey scoffed.

"Well, at least they got rooms," Welsh countered seriously. "They can. lay down. They don't have to sit in the hall readin' Fanny Hill."

"I keep telling you this is a good book, a historical romance, it says," Kiemey complained.

"Whatever it is, they got it better than we do," Welsh said, and departed in search of a hamburger and a cup of coffee and maybe a piece of pie if they had any lemon meringue left.

In Room 222, Walton Robinson, foreman of the jury, lay on the twin bed nearer the door and watched Juror Number Two, George Oliver, at the window. Oliver was looking out past the edge of the shade into a court, trying to find something interesting in the few-lighted windows that dotted the opposite wall.

Robinson had taken off his topcoat and hat, his suit jacket and tie, and shucked his shoes, but that was as far as he had gone toward undressing for the night. It was as far as he was going to go until Oliver made some move of his own. Damned if he, Walt Robinson, was going to strip down to his shorts until the other man at least took off his shoes Which was ridiculous, of course, this strange, suddenly come-by modesty (if that's what it really was) in a fifty-one-year-old married man who had spent four years in the Army and before that had put in eight years in preparatory school and college, living in close quarters with other men. Until just recently there had been no sign of this puritanical foolishness, but lately there had been increasingly frequent occurrences of this twisted attitude in which al! Walt Robinson's old, sane, steady values had somehow come unglued.

And never so bad as this; this man, Oliver, made Robinson desperately uncomfortable.

It could not be the other juror's looks; Oliver was a pretty run-of-the-mill specimen, not bad-looking in a dark-skinned, bright-eyed, curly-headed way, dressed conservatively enough except for an overly large initialed ring on his left hand. His talk might be sprinkled with bits of wilted humor and he might look at women, all women, too calculatingly but, Robinson reminded himself, Oliver must be younger than he by at least twenty years, and how could he, Wait Robinson, remember how he had looked at women twenty years ago?

No, there was nothing that Robinson could put his. finger on to explain his intense dislike of George Oliver. But this was nothing exactly new, either. All his life he had met men and women who had aroused uneasiness in him for no clearer reason, even if never to this degree. On too many occasions, the people who had aroused this instinctive aversion had hurt him in some way, sometimes seriously in matters involving money or by senseless slander and at other times no more importantly than by a casual incivility passed after too many cocktails or a cutting remark about some product the other person knew was an account at Walt's agency.

It had been this way ever since he could remember. When he was a kid, Robinson's father had once told him, "Walt, you can't dislike a new boy on sight. You've got to give him the benefit of the doubt till he can prove himself to be a good boy or a bad one. Time enough to say then whether you'll let him join your tree house club or not the boy who had just moved into the neighborhood (that was back in Maryland) was named Eddie Sylvester, and all the other kids in the gang had accepted him with no more than-the usual wariness a crowd of twelve-year olds shows a newcomer. As President of the club, because Pop had built the tree house headquarters in the Robinson's back yard, Walt had had the final say on whether or not Eddie could join the gang, and apparently the new boy's parents had said something to Pop about the blackball. This should have been enough to prove that Eddie was no prize, because what kind of kid squawked to his folks if he didn't get let in right away, but after Pop's ultimatum Walt said okay, Eddie Sylvester could join the Charles Avenue Tigers.

And what happened? Not more than a month later some five-year-old girl's mother tracked her missing child to the tree house on a Saturday afternoon when all the other Tigers were playing a pickup lacrosse game in "Latham's lot," and there she found Eddie doing things to the little girl, things that led to Eddie being shipped off some where to a special disciplinary school and the tree house coming down. Not that Pop or any of the other Tigers parents really thought they'd do anything like that but—well, the tree house was too dangerous, anyway; somebody was sure to fall and break an arm sooner or later.

And the closeness that had existed between Walt and his father never was quite the same after that. So maybe Eddie had talked before he was sent away and Pop knew that he, Walt, had been with Eddie during one previous experimental session in the tree house with another little girl whose mother had, not tracked her down.

Eddie Sylvester might have been crossed off as just one hunch that had proved out, had it not been for the fact that a great percentage of similar hunches, if they could be called that, had proved out almost as convincingly. Not all, but most, and now this Juror Number Two, George Oliver, had slapped Walt with a strong negative impression the first time he had seen the fellow, when the jury panel first had assembled in the bullpen. He, Robinson, had been the first juror chosen in the 'Falconetti trial, and that after two men before him had been excused and one challenged by the defense. Two more veniremen had been passed over before Oliver had been examined and accepted, so becoming Juror Number Two and, worse luck, Robinson's roommate for the night.

Lying on the hotel bed, the jury foreman wondered now Just how much his feelings toward Oliver had counted in his arguments against the other jurors' move to be locked up for the night- How much of his not-guilty votes was due to his belief that a not-guilty verdict could be reached much more quickly than a guilty verdict and so free him from Oliver's company, and not on the testimony presented him?

Some jury, Robinson told himself dismally. A man's life at stake, and maybe all the rest are voting their way on no stronger convictions than mine.

George Oliver turned back from the window and looked over the room, his nose wrinkled. "What a dump" he said. "I don't know why they couldn't put us in a decent place. The Waldorf—you can have your new places but when all's said and done there's no place like the Hilton or Hyatt I always say."

Robinson did not answer. Instead, he kept his eyes pinned on Oliver, his mouth fallen open, a chill spreading within him. Now he knew why he had disliked Oliver on sight. Now it was clear as crystal, and it was strange that he had not recognized it before this. For George Oliver—was Eddie Sylvester, grown up! The eyes, the nose, the arrogant voice, the constant posing, everything.

As he stared, Robinson went back to the tree house on that Sunday evening when he and Eddie and the little girl. He heard the cicadas droning, the muted sounds of faraway activity, out of reach, no danger to them, and he saw in every shameful detail.

"Hey," Oliver said. "You all right, Anderson?"

He came back to the present with a wrench and twisted his mouth in what he hoped was a smile. "Sorry," he said. "I just remembered something. Something—ah— something I should have done."

"Well, I was saying why couldn't they put us up in some place like the Hyatt instead of this flophouse?" Walt's voice failed him in his first attempt to speak, and he cleared his throat. "I don't think the taxpayers would appreciate that." C'mon, c'mon, Eddie had jeered. She can't hurt you.

"I would," Oliver was saying, "and I'm a taxpayer. Incidentally, Robinson, if you ever need a good taxman, let me steer you onto mine. Saves me five-ten grand a year and all legal. Or at least I haven't been sent to Prison yet."

you say anything about this and you'll go to prison, Eddie had warned when they parted.

Oliver was grinning at him and saying, "Hey, you might be an Internal Revenue snoop, for all I know. If you arc, forget I said that, will you?"

Robinson's smile arched at the corners, but he answered, "You're safe."

Oliver snapped a silver-cased lighter and blew out cigarette smoke in a thick stream. "What is your line, anyway?" he asked.

"Advertising," Robinson replied. Yes, I'm an experienced advertising account executive, a family man with a regular churchgoer and I've never done anything shameful except that one time, just that once, so help me God.

"A huckster, huh?" Oliver asked. "One of the Madison Avenue boys." Deep dark, gusty exhale. "Always thought I'd like to try that racket someday. Action. Challenge, Right down my alley." Drag, exhale. "Yup, if I wasn't doing pretty good in my own line I might be tempted to give advertising a whirl, just for kicks."

He waited for Robinson to ask him what his line was, and when the other man remained silent, he said, "I'm in securities myself."

"Oh?"

"Yeah, mutual funds."

"Oh."

"Whaddaya mean, Oh?" Oliver asked belligerently.

"Nothing. Nothing at all. I just said oh. I didn't mean anything special by it."

"Well, it sounded to me like you might have the wrong idea that a lot of people have, that mutual funds aren't real top-drawer, they're sort of door-to-door stuff," Oliver said. "If you think anything like that, I better put you straight. It's a multi-billion-dollar business these days, friend, and it's going to get bigger instead of smaller, no matter what the Harvard boys in The Street say about it."

"I don't know anything about it," Robinson said, and despised himself for his apologetic tone. "I'm strictly a savings-bank and life-insurance man myself. What say we get some sleep, eh?"

"Savings bank? Life insurance?" Oliver's voice showed his deep disdain. "You expect to make it big with a savings account and an insurance policy that could pay you off in twenty-cent dollars. Let me quote you some simple figures on—"

"No," Walt said sharply. "No, I don't want any figures or anything else except some sleep." Sleep, with this ghost in the next bed? He attempted a laugh and added, "I'm sorry, Oliver but I'm bushed. I should think you would be, .too."

"Me, bushed? Hell, no. Just show me a blonde and a bottle of booze and I'll show you how bushed I am. Speaking of blondes, how about that Alspach dame? A real dish, huh, and strictly on the promote, believe you me." He went on to describe the Alspach woman's physical perfections, one by one, and then explained exactly how he would enjoy a "session" with her, when the time came.

"Look, I'm pretty tired" Walt said desperately. "How about knocking it off and hitting the sack, Oliver?"

"Sure, sure, be right with you."

Oliver wandered back to the window and peeked around the side of the shade again. "They sure got a dead house here tonight. Hardly a light and the only shade that's up is an old guy watching TV." He turned to sweep the room with his bright black eyes. "How come we didn't rate a TV?" he asked. "Fine thing; here we're giving our valuable time on the jury and they're too chintzy to give us a TV."

He crossed to the telephone, and Robinson asked) "What are you going to do now?"

"Get a TV sent up here, that's what I'm going to do," .Oliver replied. He hammered at the bar of the phone cradle.

"We don't want a TV," Robinson protested. "Besides, I don't think they let Jurors have them, any more than newspapers."

"What are they, afraid of the late late movie?"

"You. know, I been meaning to say something before this," Oliver said, "but haven't I met. you somewhere before?"

"The foreman tried to keep his tone light.

"No, I don't think so," he said. He walked around the foot of Oliver's bed to the far side of his own and got in, reached over to shut off the bed lamp between the two.

"Hey, aren't you. going to open the window?" Oliver asked. "I can't sleep without a window open."

"The air conditioning—"

"In this trap? Hell, we'd wake up sluggier than we went to bed." He bounded up and padded across the floor to fling up the window, paused to lean over the sill and crane his head to the left, in the general direction of the room that housed the dish, Ann Alspach. He could not possibly have seen anything, but he made a juicy smacking sound before he drew in his head and returned to bed.

"That's all I need right now," he announced. "A young piece of tight skin like Aispach. How about it, Robinson? I bet you get your share. You Madison Avenue guys are dogs with the women, according to what I've seen in the movies. Rock Hudson, he's always a big advertising man with a string of women."

"I'm afraid it's a little different in real life," Robinson said. "Good night."

"Not talking, hub? Well, I always say a little playmate on the side never hurt anybody, so long as you don't take it too seriously. Play the field, that's me, and as soon as a dame starts getting serious, tie the can to her quick."

"Good night."

Oliver laughed. "Don't mind me," he said. "I just got that Alspach girl on my mind. I happen to like women, that's all." He turned on his side with a creak of springs and a rustle of bedclothes. "Good night, Robinson." And then, after a long pause, "You're sure we never met anywhere before this?"

Walton Robinson, saw Eddie Sylvester's bright eyes peering, heard Eddie's snicker and the juicy smacking sound he'd made with his lips. "Positive," he said firmly. "Good night, Oliver."

Later, with Oliver snoring faintly, Robinson, foreman of the 'Falconetti jury, lay in torment while the vision of Linda, his seventeen-year-old daughter's best friend in high school, taunted and cajoled him with. impossibly pritrient gestures from the foot of the bed.

I'm going crazy, Robinson told himself again. I ought to have myself locked up before I disgrace Muriel and the kids by doing something hideously vile.

And still later: No, I'm just overtired and I only imagined that Oliver looks like Eddie and all his talk about that Alspach woman—no, it's just a bad dream, or a half dream, anyway. Linda? I feel toward her as I do toward my daughter, not a bit of—of—that other. Not a speck. But, ah, Linda's so...

CHAPTER THREE

While George Oliver bad been complaining to the night phone operator about the lack of a TV in Room 222 of the Hotel Inness, Assistant District Attorney Charles Wolfe sat before his set in the den of his split-level suburban home and watched the late news.

Wolfe took his shoes off and propped his feet up on a needle point stool in front of the dilapidated leather chair that his wife, Elizabeth, had threatened times without end to give to the Goodwill collectors the very next time they hit Elm Terrace. Beth was saving trading stamps to get Charley one of those new three-way recliners, but the going was slow. Charley was hell for trading with the little fellows, the mom-and-pop stores in their burb, rather than with the supermarkets that gave stamps, and it took forever to fill one book, not to speak of the forty-five she would need for a recliner.

Elizabeth Wolfe was apt to complain about Charley's quixotic defense of the doomed little stores in their struggle against the supermarkets, but she could understand it. Grandpa Wolfe had owned a successful meat market in his day, and one of the giants had come in almost across the street and there went the market, plus all Grandpa Wolfe's savings, wasted in a futile attempt to survive. Ever since then Charley would rather do without than buy at a supermarket, even the weekend specials that would have spread the house money so much further, with trading stamps.

Her friends said, "If Charley was my husband and tried to make me deal at those grotesque little stores,

And although she never said it aloud, Beth's silent reply was always. But Charley's not your husband; he's mine, thank our kind and loving Lord, he's mine!"   Married thirty-six years and still as much in love as the day she walked down the aisle to marry him, that was Elizabeth Wolfe, and in her suburban set she sometimes considered herself some kind of a nut. Her friends were forever running off to psychiatrists and marriage counselors to find ways of "improving their husband-and-wife relationships," a few engaged in affairs or Elizabeth was almost sure they did; they all but boasted about them, and since they had built this house and moved out from the city, three couples in the immediate neighborhood had split up, two Nevada divorces and a permanent separation.

Now, as she brought in a tray of tea and sandwiches, Beth looked at Charley and felt a twinge of love and sympathy. He looked so tired, so discouraged, and that was because the 'Falconetti jury hadn't come right back in with the guilty verdict he had worked so hard for. She knew from experience that her husband mistrusted locked up Juries; in all his career as Assistant D.A. only one or two such juries had finally voted for conviction.

The TV was saying, ". . . the fire was brought under control only an hour ago. Estimated property damage is well over four million dollars."

In the pause that followed this announcement, she asked, "Do you want lemon or cream in your tea, dear?"

He raised a hand and said, "Hold it a second, will you, please?" and she put the tray down on the table across the den, pushing aside the stack of books she had brought home from the lending library that afternoon, two Mysteries a shocker her friends had told her she simply must read, especially the part that began on page 112, and a nonfiction dealing with Biblical archaeology, the Dead Sea Scrolls, and things like that. When she got around to this last volume, after the mysteries and the shocker, she would fret over the money due on the lot and the time that would be required to read a thick book with such fine print, so she would return the "cultural" nonfiction unread. Later, she would mention the fact that she had found the book in the lending library and would advise her friends not to miss it; it started slow but it was fascinating once one got into it. She

40

had done this more than once in the past, and these incidents represented almost the full extent of Elizabeth Wolfe's duplicity in life.

The TV was saying, "The Vitto 'Falconetti jury is still out. The eight men and four women who are obligated to decide whether 'Falconetti lives or dies are quartered for the night in a hotel near the courthouse. They will resume deliberations at nine ayem on the spectacular murder case."

A pause and then, "In basketball tonight, the New York Knicks topped the Boston Celtics 121 to 110 and—" There was a stark silence, the shrinking dot of the picture tube, as Wolfe snapped off the set with a grunt.

"I'm sorry," Beth. said. "Lemon?" When her husband motioned, she forked a slice of lemon into his cup and passed it to him, then handed him a plate of sandwiches. He took a paper-thin deviled ham and looked at it with a benign sort of acid amusement "I see the—and I quote—girls were in for bridge."

"What?" she asked. "Oh, the sandwiches. Well, we had quite a few left over and I thought you'd be hungry. At least it's not cucumber."

"Tastes good," Charley said after he swallowed his first bite. "We don't happen to have any Liederkranz in the house, do we? And a can of beer?"

"No," Elizabeth lied," and besides, you can't afford indigestion tonight, not with the jury still out. Eat up all the nice dainties and drink your tea, and tomorrow night I'll give you knockwurst and sauerkraut for dinner, with a big schooner of beer. Even cocktails before dinner. We'll celebrate, shall we?"

"I hope we have a reason to celebrate," Wolfe said glumly. He looked at the blank TV screen again and asked, "I wonder how they feel about"

"Who, dear?"

"Who? Why, the jurors, of course."

41

Elizabeth shrugged her shoulders. They were slender, rounded shoulders, probably her best feature. She might have gone a bit wide in the hips, but she'd put her shoulders and her bosom up against any woman's her age. Which, God help her, would be fifty-five in another month.

"Oh, them," she said. "Who knows anything about juries? as you always say. And how come they never say your name on television, Charley? The judge, the wonderful Troyers, even the jury foreman, what's-his-name, Robinson, and never a word about my Charley."

"What could they say about me?" he asked. "Assistant District Attorney Charles F. Wolfe waited in his den, supremely confident that the jury would hand down the verdict he fought so brilliantly to achieve, guilty of murder in the first degree. He drank his tea with lemon and ate sissy sandwiches which his wife's—and we quote—girlfriends couldn't eat because they were too busy gabbing."

Placidly she said, "Someday you're going to forget to put that, and I quote in front of the word 'girls' or 'girlfriends' and the skies are going to fall right in on us, Honestly!" She sipped her tea and went on. "And the TV wouldn't have to say all that about you, but they could at least mention your name."

"Yeah, they could probably ask, 'Any relation to Nero Wolfe?'"

"Yuk, yuk," she said solemnly. "It happened again, just the other day. A salesgirl. She thought she was the funniest thing since they invented humor."

"What did you say?"

"I gave her the old blank stare, the freeze." She sipped,,,,, her tea." It had about as much effect on her as nothing. Someday we'll have to sit down and think up a really good answer. A blockbuster." She hesitated and added, "Anyway, I think he's guilty."

Through the years, Charley had becomes adept at following his wife's thought processes, sometimes through much more convoluted always than this. "Why do you?" he asked.

"Well, I don't know," Elizabeth admitted. "I suppose because you wouldn't have prosecuted him if he wasn't guilty." She watched Charley raise his cup to his lips, and after he had sipped she said, quietly, "Look out, it's hot."

Wolfe gasped and swore as the tea parboiled his mouth, but he did not ask Beth why she hadn't warned him before he drank. She never did tell him the tea was too hot or the water at the lake too cold or the salt cellar top loose until after he had scalded his mouth, dived into below-zero hell, .or ruined his steak. Sometimes Wolfe dimly wondered if this might not be the result of a subconscious hostility but he loved Beth too much to pursue the possibility very far.

"I mean," his wife was saying, "you prosecuted him for first degree murder and you did your best to win. If you do win and you will he'll most likely die. You must think he's guilty. So if you do, I do."

"That's simple enough," Charley said, nodding.

"How about an asparagus roll? They're good, they really are."

"No, thanks. Any more deviled ham?

"No but the asparagus rolls are good, Charley. Just try one."

He took an asparagus roll and chewed it unenthusiastically as his wife asked, "Well, isn't the whole question " simple enough?"

"I'd love my job and my life if it were," Wolfe said heavily.
    She looked at him, round-eyed in alarm. There was a silence before she asked, "Well, don't you? Love your job and your life, I mean?"

He hesitated, and she rushed on. "Your life—do you mean you're unhappy, Charley? Outside your office? Have I failed yon somewhere?" A stricken look came over her face. "Charley, there's nobody else, is there?" she cried.

"For God's sake, Beth, stop talking nonsense," he told her. "When I said Id love my life more if things were simpler I just meant that if everything were black and white, yes or no, I wouldn't have the doubts I have."

"You have doubts?" she asked. "Oh, poor Charley. Have they been riding you again about your conviction percentages? Have they?"

"No, they haven't," Wolfe interrupted. "And stop making the office sound like a pack of bloodthirsty Baboons who begin howling the minute People lose a conviction. It's not like that, at all. Whatever doubts I have are about my qualifications for the rolls I find myself in. I mean if 'Falconetti wins an acquittal, will that mean another man could have gotten him what he deserves? On the other hand, who am I to argue so eloquently that twelve ordinary, impressionable human beings decide to send another human being to his death, mostly because I happened to be in good form that day?"

"You mean you don't want 'Falconetti to die? Is that it?"

He hesitated again before he nodded. "Sure, I want him to die. He deserves to die. But it would be a great pleasure if it were someone else who arranged to kill him."

She picked up a sandwich and nibbled at it, not tasting it, her brows down, her blue eyes troubled. She wanted to reassure Charley in this hour of travail, but she didn't   know what to say. She was so dumb. He should have married a brain, somebody like Jeannie, her roommate at Smith, somebody who could say just the right thing to clear away all Charley's doubts.

The best she could come up with was the rather stupid question, "Do you think you're going to win?" He gave a half-laugh. "To tell you how sure I am, I went to Rita Troyer after the jury was locked up and practically asked her to get 'Falconetti to plead guilty to murder-second or manslaughter."

Her mouth made an O in her surprise. "You didn't! But can you do that with the jury still out like that?"

"As a matter of fact, I suggested that it could be done if the jury wound up hung, to save us both from having to go through another trial, but I made the inference plain enough that I'd do what I could to arrange a lesser plea even before the jury reported back."

"Can you do that, Charley? I mean, after all this time 'and with the jury given the case, can you take it away from them at this late date?"

He sighed. "Theoretically it would be Judge Cleveland who would take the case from the jury if the deal got that far he has the final say, but I'm sure he'd be willing to accept a plea to the lesser charge. From what I know about Cleveland, he doesn't feel too good about this trial, either, and he might be glad to have 'Falconetti plead and take it out of his court's hands. If the jury brings m a guilty verdict it will also be up to them to pronounce sentence, you know."

He passed his cup back to Beth. "Any more tea? That ...tasted good. Much better than beer and Liederkranz. Thanks for curbing my lowbrow gluttony, dear."

"You're welcome," she said mechanically.

"But what is it about this trial that makes it so much different from the others? I mean, you've prosecuted a lot of men, and. women, too, and you've always been sort of" well, philosophically detached when it came to winning a verdict or losing one. Why not this time?"

He took the filled cup from her and sipped it gingerly.

"Watch out, it's hot." she told him.

"I know. About the 'Falconetti case, well, everyone knows he's a rotten bastard who's done things that should have gotten him the chair a dozen times over. But hiring somebody to kill Ferriss? That's something else again. Why would 'Falconetti, who neither respects nor fears any law made by God or man, hire a loose-mouthed ex-con to do his murdering for him? And our chief witness, Herb Jaffee. he's such a louse, himself, a pathological liar if I ever dealt with one. Why would anybody in his right mind, specially a tough old pro like Vitto 'Falconetti, consider Jaffee for a job like that, knowing he'd squeal like a stuck pig the minute he was picked up, as he was bound to be?"

Elizabeth pursed her lips. "Well, maybe—this might sound silly to you, Charley, but it's just a thought—maybe 'Falconetti reasoned it all out so you'd ask yourself that question. I mean, being such a wicked man, an old pro, as you call him, maybe he thought way ahead when he decided to kill Ferriss. Maybe he knew he'd be suspected no matter how cleverly he did the killing, so he—well, reversed his field and arranged the whole thing so stupidly that everybody would say an expert like Vitto 'Falconetti would never do it like that."

Charley Wolfe looked at his wife over the rim of the mug teacup, then smiled as be lowered it. "The old Minsk-to Pinsk gambit, eh? Maybe you've got something there, pussycat, but I'm afraid it's a little late for me to use, even it I could make it convincing enough to give to a jury. They'd have trouble understanding what I was trying to get at, I'm afraid."

"I'd understand it," Elizabeth said stoutly. .

„ Charley reached out and gave her broad rear an affectionate pat. "That's because you're a good wife," he said fondly. "And how about another sandwich, even cucumber?"

CHAPTER FOUR

In Room 224 of the Hotel Inness, Harold Stetler lay on his back and snored reverberatingly toward the ceiling. Stetler and Foreman Robinson had been the pair who had least welcomed the prospect of being locked up for the night. Stetler had pleaded with the others to try one more how of balloting to see if the deadlock could not be broken, but none of the jurors fell asleep faster or more completely than Juror Number Four once the lockup was a feat accompli.

Stetler's roommate, Juror Number Three, David Pepper (his colleagues thought of him as Old Man Pepper), lay on his bed, wide-eyed, knowing there would be no sleep for him except for a couple of broken snatches along about dawn. He slept poorly these nights, even in his own bed. Since Dr. Rosen had told him the truth (they told the patient the truth in these modern tunes, or at least some of the younger doctors did, whereas it used to be that the man who had It was the last to know), David Pepper had had trouble sleeping.

But not from fear. No, never that. It was, instead, as though the minutes, the seconds, were too precious to squander in sleep; they could better be used to think, remember, and rejoice. Oh, at times he worried, too, because he was only human, after all, and he had the human failing of thinking that those he would leave behind could not manage their lives quite so well without him. But these worries never held the stage for long. There ere too many rich memories, visions of the others future, to give a worry the room. it needed to develop into a big black woe.

For just think, David Pepper, born Davos Fefer, was so completely an American citizen that he had been chosen to sit on a jury that would pass on the life or death, of another American, a geboyrener Yatitee, and his ballot would carry as much weight as that of the foreman, that smart, educated Mr. Robinson.

This was the latest proof that God had been good to David Pepper. As if more proof was necessary! Wasn't it enough that his three fine sons, David and Martin and. Stephan, were all graduates of the university, two of them at the top of their professions? The middle one, Martin, wrote papers for his head doctors association that were the most brilliant of all those read at the conventions. And Stephan, with his big suite of offices and the appointment book filled up two months ahead, twenty dollars just for a single extraction, but more than the money even, the respect that the other dentists—-dental surgeons, really; there was a big difference—showed him. Dave—well, Dave was happy and that was the main thing. Some men were meant to be a big success in the world about them, and others were meant to make their own world in which to succeed on their own terms. So Dave had to scrimp along on about what Stephan paid his receptionist? So he wouldn't have it any other way. Take Dave away from his brushes, and his tubes of paint and he would be miserable, even making as much money as Stephan and Martin put together. Dave didn't really have any need for money he had the joy of painting pictures he believed were important even if not many other people thought so.

As far as his daughter, Rebecca—Bea—was concerned, there was no reason to be unhappy about her, either, not really. Even if she was divorced and she smoked too much and drank too many Martinis too early in the afternoon, at lunch, even, she had three wonderful children, David Pepper's grandchildren, and someday she would find herself and have the peace of mind she deserved. Meanwhile, she lived with him and ran his household even more smoothly than poor Freda had ever been able to, after all that money started coming in. Freda had never learned how to treat servants; she offended them, antagonized them without meaning to, or was so friendly toward them that they became gloykhgiltik about their work. Freda was afraid of them, that was her trouble, just as she'd been afraid of all her sons' and daughter's fine friends who came to the fine new apartment after they moved uptown lo a fashionable address.

Yes, perhaps Freda had been lonesome in her last years, yearning to go back to her old friends in surroundings where she was comfortable, but there had been happiness for her, too, in seeing her children flourish and succeed beyond their most daring dreams.

So why would David Pepper allow a doctor's truth to spoil all this accumulated happiness? He was dying? Phui, didn't all men die? He, had lived sixty-six good years (if some of them had been a struggle, that made

48

appreciation of the others that much sweeter), and he was never out to be a skull capped patriarch, sitting around the temple and arguing philosophy; he had neither the brains nor the ibertsaygllftg for-that As for the pain that probably would come before the end, he had suffered pain in his lifetime, pain of heart, and pain of body, and he had learned that a man never remembered the body pain for very long after it had passed. And besides, Dr. Rosea was a close friend of Martin's, and he had promised him that everything, would be done to make it as easy as possible at the very end.

The man on the bed beside him gave a retching snore and awoke with a gasp, choked, coughed, turned his head on the pillow, eyes wide, trying to identify this place in which he found himself

Finally, Harold Stetler sat up in bed and reached for the pack of cigarettes he had put, on the nightstand within, easy reach. The flare of his lighter reflected the shine of David Pepper's eyes, and Stetler asked, "Did I wake you up with my damned snoring? I'm sorry. I should have warned you."

"You didn't wake me up," Pepper said softly.

"Never let you get to sleep, eh?" Stetler dragged at his cigarette, the glow illuminating the craggy lines of his face. "That's the main reason I argued against being locked. up. I knew whoever had to bunk: in with. me would have a miserable night. I have this gadget at home that's supposed to stop my snoring but it doesn't work, according to my wife. Harriet." He gave a short, rueful laugh. "It's been separate bedrooms for her and me ever since the honeymoon."

He got out of bed and crossed the floor to the bathroom, the half-light from the window showing a thick-set, slightly bowlegged man in drooping shorts, his tousled head set at a cocky, aggressive angle even. at this hour and with. Stetler befogged by steep.

When he returned to his bed, Stetler sat on the edge and puffed his cigarette moodily. "Damn this jury duty, anyhow," he said finally. "Up till now I've always been able to gel out of it, one way or another, and this one time, when I really couldn't afford to give up the time, I get caught right by the short hair. Big deal I've been working or for nearly a year has to be- nailed down and I have a partner who's bound to blow it, but good, if I'm not there,"

"That's too bad," Old Man Pepper said. He did not say what he wanted to say, that the privilege of doing one's duty, as an American citizen was bigger than any other big deal ever conceived. Stetler would not understand. Such sentiments, he had been warned by his son and Rebecca—Bea—constituted flag waving, and flag waving was' square.

Mr., Pepper hastened, to reassure himself, that any of his children loved their country less than he did himself. Dave had been in The Navy during the war and had been wounded off Anzio, so badly that be walked with a limp ..that was almost a hobble, and the other two boys, too young for the war, had put in their required time in the Army between college and medical school even though they probably could have managed deferments. As for Bea, she served on more anti-communists, anti-Fascist, anti everything- for-American committees than a person would believe possible. And the time, one of her friends, a woman who should have known better, said that democracy was on its way out, that we'd be better off with what she called a "benign dictatorship," hadn't Bea practically ordered her out of the house?

Stetler half-turned on the bed and peered through the windows. "How come they took you?" he asked bluntly.

"I mean, you're not an old man or anything like that (I'm not?) but I've noticed how sick you look sometimes, how tired you get. I mean, couldn't you get your doctor to write a letter asking them to excuse you?"

Dr. Rosen had screamed and threatened when he had first found out what his patient intended to do, serve on a jury, but Pepper did not mention this. Dr. Rosen always treated him as though he were a thousand and ten years old and, besides, in the end he had shrugged his shoulders and said, "I don't know how it can hurt you if you don't get overtired, "zeyde," and it might even do you some good, as proud as you are about the whole thing."

Well, David thought, he had reason to be proud; this was achievement after so many heart breaking failures. In the old country before everybody went crazy, he had been a well-read, passably intelligent person with as much schooling as a boy of his class got in the town where he grew up. Perhaps the horrors that had followed had done something to his mind or perhaps it was just age, m any case what he had considered a matter of course, passing his naturalization examinations, had turned out to be something entirely different.

Yes, he had waited too long. He should have begun. work on this all-important development at once, as soon as he reached the United States. But first he had mistakenly tried to patch together the shreds of his former existence, to transplant the "Davos Fefer" who had been to this new country, intact, and when he had found this impossible, there had been the task of building a whole new life, a new personality, a new means of survival, and then progress and finally prosperity. This had taken time (although looking back on it, all this was really not half so important as the thing he had shirked, his naturalization), and when he first went to Americanization classes to perfect his English and learn something of his new country's laws and history, he bad found himself the schlemiel" of the whole class.

Three times he had taken his examinations, and three times he had failed. The Amendments to the Constitution had been his worst stumbling block; he would have everything letter perfect, and then when it came time to give the answers his mind would go blank again. The fact that his children would tell him he knew more about the Constitution than they did had been no comfort. There had been times when he despaired of ever getting his final papers, times when he had prayed on his knees to be freed of the tied tongue and the blank brain that overcame him when it came time to give the answers.

And finally, on the fourth try, he, David Pepper who had been 'Davos Fefer', had passed and been accepted as a citizen of the United States at a ceremony in which a judge had spoken stirring, unforgettable words about the citizen's duty to his country. Voting for the first this had been a wonderful thing, but when the jury summons had come by certified mail, that had been the culmination of it all. Now he was a citizen in the truest sense of the word because- he had been chosen to serve with other Americans to sit in Judgment of one of their peers.

Try to be excused? Did a man ask to be excused from the realization of his highest, ambition? "No," David Pepper told Harold Stetler. "No, I didn't get a doctor to write a letter." He hesitated; he didn't want to seem guilty of striking a pose. "I didn't want to be excused, you see," he said, finally. "I—I'm sorry if this sounds square, as my sons say, but I felt it a privilege to serve on this jury."

Stetler looked at him in the gloom, then returned his gaze to his cigarette. "Well, yeah, I guess it's better than the way they have it in some places," he said grudgingly, "if it only hadn't come at such a damned bad time for me." Another pause and he jerked out a laugh. "I guess if I hadn't missed out all those, other times when it really didn't make much difference, I wouldn't have been caught when it did hurt, huh? So you might say I've got myself to blame."

He crushed out his cigarette in the tray, laughed again. "And boy, I certainly got stuck with a pip, didn't I?" he asked. "Vitto 'Falconetti, of all people. The big wheel himself. Who'd ever think that I'd have a hand in deciding whether Vitto 'Falconetti would go to the chair or walk free?"

Old Man Pepper said nothing. This couldn't be called discussing the case, exactly.

Stetler said, almost to himself, "It didn't come to me till it was too late, but I bet I could have got myself challenged off this Jury. My wife, Harriet, went to the same college as 'Falconetti's wife. Not at the same time, but they belonged to the same alumnae association once. The place was the

Maryland College for Women, and it's gone down the pipe since and the alumnae association with it, I guess, but I bet if I'd remembered I could have worked it so I wouldn't have to sit on this jury and get locked up tike this."

David Pepper remained silent. He hoped this was nothing he should report to some official in the morning. Would something like this cause a mistrial if it became known? That would be terrible, to have David Pepper's one chance to do a service for his new country end in a mistrial, a stalemate.

"What was her name before she married 'Falconetti?" Stetler was musing. "Louise Somebody. Louise or Laura, I'm pretty sure."

Chapter Five

Louise Parsons 'Falconetti threw back the covers and Snapped on the lamp beside her bed, pushed her feet into slippers, and reached for a peignoir that was draped over the chair beside the bed.

She might as well give up: she wouldn't sleep all night unless she took two or three Seconal, and they left her groggy the next morning. And tomorrow morning—this morning—was one time when she didn't want to be groggy, not it. The jury came in with the verdict.

The Investigator Mr. Arlaud had called her as soon as the judge had ordered the jury locked up for the night. She had wanted to stay in the courtroom, to be with Vitto during these terrible hours, but he had said no.

"I don't know much about juries, but this bunch looked as though they were going to take their own sweet time about getting anywhere," Vitto had told her. "You know how I get when. You're around while I'm sweating something out, Lou: I have twice as hard a time, watching you suffer."

When he said this, Vitto had shown no indication that he was sweating anything out at all, not the slightest sign. He had withdrawn into that unapproachable, invulnerable superiority of his that had on occasion made her so damned mad that she could scream, as much as she loved him. The great Vitto 'Falconetti; nobody could touch him, nobody could hurt him, the world could adjust itself to conform with his desires and plans and attitudes, or the world could go to hell—that was how he seemed when he was like this. And during all her twenty-six years of being married to Vitto, she had never decided positively whether this was a pose assumed while he was experientially the normal human reactions to crisis inside himself or whether he was endowed (or damned) with a special egocentric bulwark that actually made him feel that he was inviolately superior to all the violence and confusion that swirled about him.

She reached for her cigarettes, stayed her hand, and, shook her head. No, a glass of warm milk was supposed to be good for sleeplessness (Good for terror, too, good for the panic that waited in the wings)? And this would be a fine time to put it to the test. Herbert and Violanda were sound asleep by this time and so her kitchen was hers; she probably couldn't find anything she needed and Violanda would surely give her hell in the morning when she found the kitchen messed up, but she had to do something, if only burn a saucepan of milk.

She stood up and moved toward the door, and as she did, a pier glass caught her reflection, making her pause. Perhaps this wasn't the right time to preen before a mirror, but she had to know how she looked. Had the strain of the trial made an old hag of her? Was every damned line and sag showing? Was her figure as far-gone to pot as she suspected, unbolstered by girdle and bra? Did her hair tell everybody, including her hairdresser? Was Vitto's coolness in the face of this terrible thing just a reflection of his indifference to her, the wife grown old and saggy, ready for discard?

She threw back the peignoir and examined herself critically. The light was none too good, but she was not brave enough to risk putting on more lamps. There had been a time 40,000 years before when she had deliberately sought bright sunlight to illumine her flawless complexion, when she had never given a thought to whether a room was too brightly lighted, but it was hard to remember those times. Now she instinctively sought the shadows and gave the bright places to younger women, the mere children who didn't half-appreciate the treasures of youth the smooth, firm skin, the flat bellies, the clean-lined legs and, above all, the hands that had yet to betray their owner's desperate efforts to smother the years with beauty treatments, face lifts, and other losing battles they would fight before they were through.

Not, she told herself, that she was an old hag. Not yet. Her neck was still pretty good, a little corded from dieting, and her shoulders weren't bony, not really. The trouble was, when she dieted (When had she not been dieting in the past ten years?), instead of the pounds coming off her thighs and derriere and middle, they dropped off her shoulders and neck, giving her a scrawny look in any kind of décolletage, necessitating giveaway bits of business around the neckline. Giveaway to another woman, anyway, and probably to Vitto; in spite of everything, his background, his business, the tough crowd he had to deal with, Vitto had a matchless eye for women's clothes, and for women—other women.

She shook her head again and resumed her inspection of the figure in. the pier glass. Her breasts, thank God, were very good, round and upstanding, and this was important because long ago she had learned that men were divided into two basic groups, the leg men and the breast men, and Vitto was no leg man. Not that her legs were too bad, either; there were no varicose veins or anything like that, and if her ankles were not the trimmest in the world, she could afford shoes that flattered them.

Thank the good Lord that Vitto had so much money. If they had been poor or even middle income and she had had to wear off-the-rack clothes and cheap shoes, and she couldn't afford the massages and facials and other two-hundred-a-week attentions of Karee's operators, she would be a bag and Vitto probably would be long gone.

She wrapped the peignoir about her with both hands and shivered at the thought, then reproved herself for thinking it. Oh woman of little faith, why are you so sure Vitto doesn't love you for yourself, Lou Parsons? Why did the black thought persist that Vitto had married her and stayed married to her for no other reason than that she had been a beautiful girl, a head turner, from a first line Baltimore family, somebody to show the world that he, Vitto 'Falconetti, had arrived? When had Vitto, by the slightest word or most insignificant gesture, ever shown her that he didn't love her? But then, on the other hand, when had he last shown her that he did?

She left the bedroom and went down the hall to the curving staircase that descended to the living room with its two-story glass wall, beyond which a few lights still blinked in the blackness, despite the hour. A button switch gave life to three table lamps (muted, of course) below and brought into view the decorative excellence of the apartment's central room.

Louise paused at the head of the heavily carpeted stairs and admired the room from above; she had so few opportunities really to appreciate it, to relish her few little victories over that Gay decorator and be secretly glad he had refused to give in to some of her ideas that would not have been as good as his, as it turned out. The apartment had been photographed for several status magazines, and pictures of her had been taken sitting on the semicircular sofa, holding a cigarette and smiling sweetly for $3,000, payable to the proverbial "favorite charity," some organization that helped mentally retarded children and that Fran Mcinro had sworn was both needy and worthy. (Louise had no "favorite charities" she wrote checks when she was solicited, but she was too busy being Vitto 'Falconetti's wife to work actively for any cause). She descended the stairs and went through the living room, the adjoining dining room, the butler's pantry, and on into the kitchen. It was as she had feared; Violanda had hidden all the saucepans, locked them up somewhere where only Violanda could find them, so Louise settled on a glass of cold milk in a fluted crystal goblet, which she carried back to the living room. Once there, she carefully deposited the glass of milk on a coffee table and-went to the bar in the smallish "family room," where she poured herself a large helping of Scotch and seasoned it with lukewarm soda, not daring to return to the kitchen for ice for fear she wouldn't be able to find where Violanda had hidden the refrigerator.

She sipped her drink, made a face, and went to the curved sofa on which she had been photographed. The soft lights were still too bright for her mood, so she got up again and turned off all but one in a far corner. She went back to the sofa, took another sip of the drink she had made, and found it quite palatable. That was one thing about good Scotch: it almost tasted good without ice.

It had been gin, without ice or soda or any other mixer, gin right out of the bottle, that Vitto 'Falconetti had fed her the first night she ever saw him. That was at Lutherville, outside Baltimore, where the Maryland College for Women was once situated, and from which she, Lou Parsons, had been about to graduate that June.

There were. a great many rules at that school, and one of them was that no girl, under any circumstances, would sit out a dance with a boy in his car. There was no restriction against drinking raw gin out of the boy's bottle, once parked, the rulemakers at the Maryland College for Women obviously never having conceived of such a thing happening, but if there had been it would not have deterred Lou Parsons any more than the- no-parking thing. Because Lou Parsons was a Baltimore Parsons, the top of everything in her graduating class, grades, scholastic activities, and social prominence, and she had been brought up to view rules as something required by people whose name was not Poultney or Garrett or Warbeld or Parsons.

Actually, she was not a bitch—or not exactly, anyway. She was just used to having her own way, and she had the brain and the charm to make her way more reasonable, more to be desired, than any counter course she might run up against at the college she was adored by the other girls (sometimes embarrassingly so, and at least twice to the point of requiring physical repression of an oddball gone berserk with misdirected passion) and hardly less warmly regarded by her teachers, whom she somehow patronized and treated with respect, both in the same breath.

Everybody had predicted that Lou Parsons would make her mark in the world in any field she might choose, and if she gave it any thought, Louise herself no doubt envisioned a future in which she would keep on having her own way, attaining any success she sought and eventually settling down in the Green Spring Valley with a big house, a stable of hunters, a handsome, attentive husband, and a flock of beautiful, well-behaved children.

And now she sat alone, drinking Scotch without ice and wondering if her husband, who was on trial on charges of hiring a gunman to murder a one time friend, loved her, had ever Joyed her.

It was ridiculous, insane, but no more unbelievable than what had happened to her the first time she had laid eyes on Vitto 'Falconetti. Elsa Farwea's date had brought him along as a blind date for Elsa's gruesome roommate, and how Elsa's friend had ever gotten to know a man like Vitto 'Falconetti was one of those involved things that don't make sense even when they are exhaustively explained. So never mind how he had come to Lutherville; it was enough that he came. More than enough, because his coming had wrecked Lou Parsons self-assured poise and had plunged her into an emotional turbulence from which she had yet to ever fully emerge.

"Holy cow," somebody beside her had breathed that June night in Lutherville. "Who's the glah-glah-glah by the door?"

Louise had turned, and her eyes met Vitto's squarely as his head turned in her direction, as though this whole thing had been timed by a stop watch. For a long time (two seconds, five?) they looked at each other, and for the first time in her life Louise found herself intensely attracted to a man on sight. More than that, this was no objective appreciation of a man's good looks, no cool evaluation of his clothes and his haircut and other signs of good breeding; this was a gripping, compelling need to speak to this man, touch him, know who he was and tell him who she was, to seize this moment and extend it, develop this first silent communication into the relationship that surely must be intended.

Oh yes, years later Etzio Pinza sang a song that embodied something of what Louise had felt that night, but even Hammerstein's lyrics sung by that glorious voice could impart only a fragment of her reaction, as she remembered it so later, when she met him and they found themselves in his car, she asked him who—he—was... what—he—did... and he said, I'm a bricklayer." She laughed and said something about bring serious, and he, said he wasn't kidding, exactly. "I used to lay brick, as a matter of fact. Now I'm in brickwork contracting and wholesale supply."

"A bricklayer," Mama wailed when Louise announced that she was going to marry Vitto 'Falconetti. "A common laborer." And all Lou's patient, exasperated, and finally enraged efforts to convince Mama that Vitto wasn't a bricklayer who carried a hod up a ladder failed to change her mother's opinion one-iota. No Parsons was present at the marriage held in the Elkton minister's tacky front room, and until they died, Mama one year later, and Papa in two years later, neither of her parents ever saw Vitto or forgave Louise, not even to the point of visiting her in the hospital or writing her a note when she lost the baby, six months after they were married.

But that was all right. She was able to stand the hurt of her parents' alienation, her friends' ostracism, because, being with Vitto was enough. She did not know how wealthy he was when she married him, she never dreamed that he would get to be a multi millionaire in a breathlessly short space of time, but even if he had been a common laborer carrying a hod she—no.

She sipped and shook her head. No, she had to be honest: she was never made to be a poor man's wife. She might have loved Vitto as a poor man, but she could not have stayed married to him; it would have grieved her to have to leave him, but she would have left, gone back to her family and old friends if they would have received her—and they would; she would have made them —if there had not been money to spend to alleviate her loneliness.

For she had been lonely, at first. Vitto's business required him to be away so much, not out of town but circulating in areas where she would have been not only unwelcome but miserable as well nearly every night it seemed, there was somebody Vitto had to meet at dinner, and later there were other meetings, secretive, under-the counter deals to be consummated, labor bosses to be dealt with, builders to be brought into line when they strayed a field in search of competitors' brick, city officials to be entertained, strange men from some strange office known as the Department of Weights and Measures who had to be assured they were the most delightful companions Vitto 'Falconetti could want for a night on the town, bulk suppliers to be cajoled, sweetened, threatened--there were hundreds of these shadowy figures so important to Vitto's continued success, and most of them could not afford to be seen in public with him, much less in any social circle in which the charming Mrs. 'Falconetti might move.

So she had to find her way into a circle, and- she did. A high-priced social secretary helped wedge an entree into a fairly high stratum of San Francisco society, but Lou's own talents had been responsible for her social success after that. Now she could include some of the oldest names in California on her invitation lists, and if Vitto was seldom at her side when she attended the horse show or the opera or a first night, why, it was understood that Mr. 'Falconetti was so busy getting richer that he could not afford to spend the time away from his particular arena, and not only was he forgiven but his dedication was applauded.

And then, almost out of nowhere, there appeared on the scene Dan Ferriss, another leader of the brickwork industry but one who did not seem to have to work particularly hard to be almost as successful as Vitto 'Falconetti. While Lou's husband devoted eighteen hours a day to his work, seven days a week, Dan Ferriss appeared to spend no time at his business that could interfere with his pursuit of pleasure. Dan had many of Vitto's qualities, the same rugged good looks, the massive frame, the wise eyes, but he was Vitto's opposite in many ways, too. He laughed easily, he paid little, natural compliments to women, he liked (or. professed to like) such things as chamber music and abstract art, and he had a wit that was never brilliantly cruel at another's expense, as Vitto's usually was.

Vitto and Dan were supposed to be business rivals but actually they were close friends—or at least as close as Falconettie's ever permitted a friend to become—and Louise suspected that they were more partners in a two-man cartel than actual competitors. Vitto never said so in as many words, but every indication was that whenever a big job came up for bids, Dan and Vitto joined forces in making it virtually impossible for any of the smaller fry to underbid either 'Falconetti Builders Supply or Ferriss Materials, one or the other. Whatever loss Vitto might take on an unrealistically low bid, Ferriss would share, and vice versa, and if the occasion arose when a brash new comer to the field needed chastening (truck breakdowns, scaffolding accidents, things like that), this was.." taken care of by an imported company of goons whose expenses were met by a Joint 'Falconetti-Ferriss war chest or at least this was what Louise figured out for herself from bits and pieces of Vitto's telephone conversations she overheard.

Vitto never volunteered any information or even answered her questions about his business affairs- "It wouldn't interest you," he would say. Or, "When I'm with you I don't want you asking if I've got the Mac Murray boys in hand yet or how that strike is affecting me—-I just want you to be you,"

Which was as close as he had ever come to an endearment in the latter years. Oh, Louise supposed their "love life," as Mama would have called it, was satisfactory or at least on a par with that of her friends, if not better than most. At least she didn't have to run to an analyst about it. As not a few of her friends did. But softness, helplessness in love, the slightest dependence on her—what kind of man had she thought she was marrying that day in Elkton, a poet?

61

Yes, everything had been fine up to about two years ago, when Vitto started to grow cold and distant, even more detached than he had been from the start. Not in any way she could put her finger on, even now. He was always courteous, always pleasant, but the times when he said, "Drop by my room after your shower; I've got something to show you," grew further and further apart and then stopped altogether. At first she had told herself that men, got older, as women did, that she needed no physical proof that their relationship was sound and good, and she blamed herself for putting so much importance On the lack—and then she started wondering if there was somebody else.

She knew now that she should have sought outside help for her problem. She had even gone so far as to make an appointment with a recommended analyst (a Dr. Martin Pepper) and of course there were jokes about his name and the soft drink; she wondered why he didn't change it), but she had broken the appointment at the last moment, scoffing at her own lack of self-sufficiency. If she had gone to the analyst, he might have suggested a course far different from the one she eventually had taken or had had so subtly forced upon her.

Now she finished her drink in three gulps and coughed faintly as the Scotch roughened her throat for a moment. She put down the glass beside the brimming glass of milk and shut her eyes as the forbidden memories crashed through the barriers she had set up against them, the memories of Louise Parsons 'Falconetti in the amis of Dan Ferriss, as actively and as lovelessly responsive as the most abandoned slut.

CHAPTER SIX

I've got a can of tuna fish," Gary. offered.

"In that case, I'm kidding," the Rita said. She walked to a deep chair and sat down, thrust her feet out in front of her, and leaned back her head with a sigh. "I'm a little tired," she admitted.

"Your old (She was really seven years younger than Gary) Rita is feeling her years tonight."

"Some old Rita," Gary jeered as he moved to the tiny kitchen space behind the counter and started filling a percolator with water. "Overeats like a kid home from prep school and then wonders why she feels logy." He spooned coffee into the percolator's basket. "You'd better go back to your spartan diet tomorrow—you'll need all your strength when that jury reports m that it's hung and here we go again."

Troyer covered his eyes and groaned. "Don't say such a thing. I refuse to believe it." .

Gary plugged in the coffeepot and headed for the couch that would turn into his Boss's bed for the night if she wanted. "Why , not?" he asked. "It's happened to you before."

"Well, I'll tell you why not! Because if it is a hung jury, then there'll be a new trial, and I can't face the thought of defending Vitto 'Falconetti again. That's why not."

Gary grinned as He threw back the cover of the daybed. "It was just a suggestion," he said mildly.

"It was a rotten suggestion," Rita snapped.

Rita and Gary had a strange relationship by any office standard. Rita was married to a wonderful man for twenty plus (who she loved dearly) years who had nothing to do with his wife's Law Practice and traveled extensively in the Construction industry. She said as much as 200 days a year. He always attended the Troyer Law Firm Christmas party. Gary had seen him exactly three times since 1986. It was un spoken but well established from the beginning (*See Caribbean Cops V*) that there would never be sex between them; it would ruin everything. Rita's longest serving Para Legal was named Chantel, the most independent liberated feminist girl friend Gary ever had. When Rita had a Big Case such as 'Falconetti Rita and Gary worked together hand and glove until it was over to the emotional exclusion of everyone else. The staff got orders to fill their needs and the three Associates handled all other legal work that came in. Rita lived a goodly distance away in Napa so sleepovers when it was really late were not un-common.

The PI (where was this in his job description) folded the cover and carried it to a closet to store it on a shelf, brought down. freshly laundered sheets and pillowcases. "The Jurors had over five hours to talk be fore they were taken to their hotel," he reminded his Boss . "You know what happens when certain jurors vote guilty and then the others try to make them change their minds. It's embarrassing to have to admit you're wrong in front of eleven people. They become twice as stubborn and—"

"Ya'know," Rita broke in, "I Just might go spend the night at my own house."

"Okay," Gary said, relenting, "the discussion is tabled." ,.

"Good." Rita Troyer got out of-the chair and moved to the window, looking down at the silent street below, her hands thrust in her pockets, her face thoughtful. "Sometimes I wish I'd specialized in corporate law," she said moodily.

"Oh, Lord," Gary laughed. "Don't tell me you're in that mood."

"Well, I mean it," Rita said. "In that field they deal in blacks and whites, with only an occasional shadings, of gray. In criminal law we have to handle the whole spectrum, and sometimes it gets a little confusing. Like now, for instance."

Gary looked from his bed making, his eyebrows arched. "I know this case has been a drag, perhaps the worst one we've ever had, but what's so confusing about it? I mean now, with the evidence in, and the jury locked up for the night? The jury acquits or convicts or deadlocks. Three possibilities. Where's the confusion?"

Rita sighed and turned to the chair she had just left. "I didn't tell you before because I didn't want my dinner ruined by a lot of discussion, but Charley Wolfe all but said he was willing to let 'Falconetti plead to murder

64

second or even man slaughter, in case of a hung jury or even before the jury reports in."

Gary straightened and shook his head. " Wow, I can't see our genial client doing anything like that, can you?"

Rita shrugged. "Offhand, I can't, but I never claimed to be an authority on Vitto 'Falconetti's reactions to situations. He'll have all night to Up there in his cell and wonder which way that jury's going to swing. They'll all be long hours for 'Falconetti tonight."

Well, I still don't see where there's any confusion," Gary argued. "It will be his decision to make, won't it?"

His boss nodded. "But if he asks my advice, what am I going to tell him, Gary? Take the offer and plead, and settle for ten-to-twenty years when there's a fifty-fifty chance, at least, that the jury would set him Scott-Free? Or stick by his guns, rely on his self-professed innocence, and then get life or the Gas? What answer shall I give him, Gary, if he asks me which way to decide?"

There was a brief silence, broken only by the murmur of the percolator, and then Gary said, "If past performances mean anything, the last thing in the world Vitto 'Falconetti is going to do is ask your advice. He never has, not from the first day we talked with him' in the Jail, remember?"

"Yes," Rita said soberly. "I remember."

****

When the guard brought 'Falconetti into the little conference cubicle that first day, Rita rose from her chair and measured this man she had been asked to defend, this Vitto 'Falconetti whose name she had read in a thousand newspaper stories, all having to do with big money and strife and violence, this rich man who was virtual czar of San Francisco's brickwork industry, and his first impression was that here was the toughest-souled individual she had-ever shaken hands with.

The Troyers (as Rita and Gary were a known team) had had many clients whose reputation for callousness had preceded them, but in the times of dangerous stress that had brought them to these outstanding Criminal Defense team, every one, till 'Falconetti, had sooner or later shown a flaw in the shell, had given Rita and Gary a glimpse of the human fear that lay beneath the case-hardened pose the tough guy sought to maintain All important factor in a case, particularly a murder-one case in which the clients life was at stake. Her voice was remarkably even super humanly pleasant as she told 'Falconetti, "You'll get a bill for our services, just like everybody else."

"For how much?" Vitto 'Falconetti asked bluntly.

"For One hundred twenty-five thousand dollars, not counting the possible appeal" Rita Troyer replied, with equal bluntness.

"Win or lose?" Rita nodded.

"That's right."

The accused man's-eyes had been absolutely expressionless. "That's a lot of money," he said..

"If you win, it's worth, it," Troyer explained. "And if you lose—well, you won't have very much to do with the money, anyway."

'Falconetti's wide mouth had twitched at the corners without showing any suggestion of levity. "You drive a hard bargain. Counselor."

Rita shook her head. "There's no bargain involved. That's the deal."

'Falconetti gave a hard, dry laugh. 'Take it or leave it, eh? Y'kaow, you got me at a disadvantage. It's been a long time since I had to meet a asking price."

It was Rita's turn to smile. "That's how I got to be a millionaire," She said wryly.

'Falconetti nodded. "Yeah. Me, too, Troyer, except I'm for real. You knew that, didn't you, and that's why you jumped at the chance to take the case, eh? What happened? Did O'Rourke lay it out for you, tell you how much of a fee to hit me with?"

Gary Arlaud, standing in a comer, shifted his feet and cleared his throat. Rita knew that Gary wanted him to tell 'Falconetti to call in somebody else because the big man's first few words had made it abundantly clear that there followed Gary's lead, but at the time she reminded herself that men facing the gas chamber say strange things, assume strange attitudes, out of their, inner desperation. Some of the most uncooperative, even belligerent, of them had squared around once the relationship had been established, and those who hadn't—well, the practice of Criminal law was idealistically a matter of principle above personalities, anyway.

So, although he must have blown inwardly that Vitto 'Falconetti's unfriendly attitude was genuine, no pose, and would not change with time or understanding, Rita said, "No, George O'Rourke didn't mention anything about your money, Mr. 'Falconetti. I imagine he was too distressed over your predicament to think of such a thing."

'Falconetti snorted "That'll be a day, when George O'Rourke forgets money because I'm in a jam." He lit a cigarette without offering one to either Troyer, leaned back in his straight chair, and said, "So, okay, the deal is for one hundred twenty-five thousand dollars. Where do we go from here?"

"Well, first," Rita said, "suppose you answer some questions for me." She paused and added quietly, "I don't suppose I have to remind you that if we're going to do you any good at all, you must level with us, no matter how it may hurt at times."

'Falconetti assumed .a reproachful expression so patently exaggerated as to the almost comic. "Why, Counselor, how could you think I could do anything else?" he asked.

Rita's jaw came forward and her voice was brittle. "I mean it, Mr. 'Falconetti. The man who tries to kid his Lawyer is a fool) and I take it you're no fool, whatever else may be said about you."

'Falconetti's mocking smile faded. "I'm not," he said grimly, "DO matter how much of a fool I may have sounded just now. Sorry. It won't happen again. Go ahead with your questions, Troyer."

Rita took the time to open her attaché case and find the list of questions Gary and she had prepared, even though he needed no prompter. Let him sit there for a spell and reflect on his own asymmetry and the sharp answer it got; maybe it will blunt his superiority the least bit. Which I doubt.

She uncapped her fountain pen and held it over a yellow pad. "All right, then, did you contract to have Dan Ferriss killed?"

"No," 'Falconetti said immediately.

"Next question."

"Did you know Ferriss?"

"Of course I knew him. I practically raised him in the industry, everybody knows that He was a personal friend besides being a—well, a friendly competitor, I guess you'd call him."

Rita did not raise her eyes from the pad on which she was writing. "What business?"

"Oh, come on!" the big man across the table protested. "We were fellow bricklayers. You read the newspapers, don't you?"

"Just the same, I'd like you to tell me," Rita Said.

'Falconetti hesitated, on the verge of rebelling against reciting facts that any adult, literate Californian should know. "I contract for brickwork on construction jobs. Big stuff. So did Ferriss. His company was Ferriss

Materials, Incorporated. Mine is 'Falconetti Builders Supply, also Incorporated. Mine's the bigger outfit by about fifty mil lion bucks a year, gross." He tapped his cigarette loose in a tray beside him, "Does that answer your question?"

"Yes, thanks, at least for the time being," Rita said impersonally. "Now then, do you know a man named Herbert Jaffee?"

"No, I don't. I met him in whats-his-name's office, the D.A., and so far as I know that was the first time I ever laid eyes on him."

Rita looked up quickly. The gray-green eyes were steady, neither too intent nor too unconcerned. Rita said, "The District Attorney says you paid Jaffee to kill Ferriss."

'Falconetti's wide shoulders moved in the suggestion of a shrug. "And all you have to do is prove I didn't," he retorted. "For one hundred twenty-five thousand dollars. That shouldn't be hard."

"And," Rita Troyer continued, "Jaffee says the same thing, that you paid him ten thousand dollars to kill...

"I don't care what that bastard Jaffee says, I didn't," 'Falconetti said steadily. "What more can I tell you than that I didn't, period"

Rita frowned slightly. "But if you don't know Jaffee, why would he name you?"

Another half-shrug. "There are quite a few citizens who would love to see me framed good, Rita. Maybe somebody made it worth Jaffee's while to put the finger on me, I don't know. You find out, Rita; that's why I'm paying you all. that lovely money."

Troyer put down her pen and leaned back in her chair, her mouth slanted, her eyes quizzical. "I'm curious about something, Mr. 'Falconetti," she said. "Why do you keep referring to money all the time? Since you have so much, why should it be that important to you at a time like this?"

The big man across the table ground out his cigarette with a curiously ruthless motion. "I'll tell you why, Counselor. It's because I didn't come by it easy, the way you probably did, Ms. Yale or Harvard or whatever you are.. I grew up in Hell's Kitchen, over by the wholesale meat houses, and believe me, the beef in the pens had it better than. I did before I decided I'd better do something about improving my lot, I guess you'd call it. My old man was a drunk and my mother was off in the head; maybe she was hooked on something, I don't know, but whatever screwed her up the way she was sure made her forget about all such things as mother love. Before I learned to duck real good I got my head laid open about once a week, and I'm always carrying a black eye or a split lip or a—ah, t'hell with it; you'll think I'm crying about it."

She shook her head. "I'm not, not really,"

He went on. "It's an education, y'might say. I learned real early that the guy who gives the knocks don't take so many himself."

Rita noticed that although 'Falconetti's voice was still cold and measured, his cultivated correctness of speech had begun to show a few holes with what must have been a stirring of long-smothered resentments.

"So I left home," 'Falconetti was saying. "I got to be a real hard character at an age when I guess you were going to dancing school maybe or playing post office at some highbrow birthday party where all the little boys and girls had clean necks. Me, I was scrambling, chasing the buck. I was a hoodlum, an errand boy for some hard operators, and after that I graduated to loft worker, and finally I made what was pretty big time for me. I was enforcer for a mob you probably never heard of, but it was close to the top at the time. So on the way up I stole things, I busted up things, I beat heads in, and I killed quite a few people here and there, too. But not Dan Ferriss, and the other is privileged information so you won't say anything about it, Rita, will you?"

He waited until she slowly shook her head.

70

"Then," 'Falconetti continued, "something happened, and T turned respectable as all hell. I worked my tail off at this new line, and I only had to use my disreputable experience now and then before the people who were leaning on me, trying to keep me down, let up because they got scared of me. They had a right to be; I didn't want anybody in my way and if they didn't move over, I rammed right through them, the hard way. So after this and that, I began making a lot of money and I got to be pretty important, and now you can't find a more respectable son of a bitch in town than Vitto 'Falconetti. I've got a beautiful wife from a fine family, and she takes care of the social side. I've got a duplex apartment in a good neighborhood, as good as yours if not better, and a Bentley for Lou and an Alfa Romeo that'll do a hundred and twenty-seven on the Thruway in case you like speed, and a whole flock of nice little things like that."

He brought his hand up and inspected the square tipped nails. "And the whole goddam exercise was all for money, Rita" he said, almost absently. "It was a lot tougher than becoming a lawyer, but I haven't got the equipment to be a lawyer so I had to do it my way."

"So now you're the complete success in every way, is that it?" Rita asked, just as mildly.

'Falconetti glanced up quickly from his study of his fingernails. "Was that supposed to be a crack?"' he asked. "If it was, you missed Counselor. Sure I'm a success, show me where I'm not. What do I need, besides getting out of this crazy frame that somebody put on me? What more could I possibly want?"

Gary Arlaud spoke from the corner of the little room. "Ever hear of a thing called peace of mind, Mr. 'Falconetti?" he asked.

The big man at the table spared him one contemptuous glance before he turned back to Rita. "What do you do, carry him around to come up with little bits like that?" he asked. "Peace of mind—is that supposed to mean I can't enjoy anything I got because I stepped in some faces getting it? Unh-unh, not Vitto 'Falconetti. Whatever I did, I don't worry about. If I hadn't done it to them, they would have done it to me. If I hadn't taken it from them, they'd have taken it from me. So now I've got it and that's all I want.*

He paused and added, "And I'm paying you one hundred twenty-five thousand dollars to see that I can keep on using it." Rita began putting papers back in the attaché case. Her voice kept its impersonal tone. "I find it pretty hard to be sympathetic to you, Mr. 'Falconetti," She said. "I want you to know that now, at the start."

'Falconetti laughed. "I'm not asking you to be sympathetic, Troyer. Just be brilliant—that's what I'm paying you for."

"Here's your coffee," Gary told his Boss. "Come back, come back, wherever you were."

Returned to Gary's apartment with a half start and reached up to take the steaming cup. She raised it almost to her lips, and then lowered it.

"Thinking back," She said, "I can't imagine why I Just didn't refer him to another lawyer right at the start." Gary did not turn from the breakfast bar, where he was filling his own cup. "That's easy," he said. "Deep down, you're an idealist, always thinking the best of your fellow man. You couldn't believe that 'Falconetti was, for real when you met him; you took the case so you could be there when he dropped that hard-boiled pose of his and turned human. The only thing is that it's no pose with 'Falconetti: That's the way he is, and that's the way he'll be the day he dies. Which won't be as soon as it probably ought to, if we've done a good job defending him."

Rita sipped her coffee and added, "Which we have, God help us, which we have."

CHAPTER SEVEN

In Room 226 of the Hotel Inness, Mrs. Lorraine Brown, Juror Number Five, wondered if her roommate, Elsie Harding, was sleeping soundly enough for her to risk getting the two dinner rolls she had put in her handbag at the restaurant. They were very small rolls, and if the other woman woke up she, Lorraine, would feel called upon to offer her one, and Elsie Harding looked like the kind who Would say thanks, I believe I will.

It was not, Mrs. Brown assured herself, that she was stingy; it was the principle of the thing. Elsie Harding had had as much chance to slip a couple of rolls into her bag at dinner, but oh, no, such a thing probably was beneath the snooty Miss Hardding, she and her fancy way of talking and her lah-dee-dah airs, the dainty way she ate, her rush to get right into the shower the minute they'd -reached this room, as though being with all those common people in court ail day had dirtied her.

There must be a reason she wasn't married, too. She Must be all of thirty-five but she wore no wedding ring, and Mrs. Brown's nudging questions 'about whether she was divorced had been met with a cool stare and a deliberate change of subject.

She needn't think she was so beautiful, either. At her age Lorraine Brown had had more ass than Elsie Harding, a lot more. Not that Lorraine considered herself exactly an old bag even now but, well, she was fifty-two and she'd been married to Brownie for thirty-one years, and anybody who'd lived that long with a man like Brownie was bound to get a little frayed around the edges. Not that Brownie wasn't a fine person when he was sober, one of the sweetest guys in the world, but he couldn't leave the bottle alone. A good man's failing, somebody had called it, and maybe there was something to that, but the stuff sure had made a stinker out of him real quick. When a girl's husband was in the bag most of the time, it got so that she didn't see the sense of trying to keep herself up; she quit dieting, and what difference did it make if she got a new permanent or not, or stopped scrimping to buy herself a decent dress once in a while.

And it took some scrimping, too, even to make ends meet, with Brownie not able to hold any kind of a job past the first payday, the second at most. Back then there'd been no question but that someday he'd have his own agency, and everybody knew the kind of gold mines they were. But in-a-while binge drinker into a thick-voiced stranger who lost all his laughs and his fast thinking, a zombie in the morning who had to have a half-pint, at least, before he could start to get dressed. And everything went down the tubes. What happened? Loraine Brown kept asking herself, was it something I did or didn't do? But there never was an answer, not a whisper of one.

Well, anyway, thank God, she had raised the kids to be decent citizens with a chance for everything she had missed because Brownie had blown it for booze. Lorry was married and had two darling children, and she lived out west, in Salt Lake City, where her husband, Al, had a good job, engineer for a big company that had something to do with uranium. Junior wasn't married yet, but he was going with a nice girl and maybe this was the one. He didn't come to see her any more, just called up, and maybe it was better that way because it was ten to one if he came to the house he'd get in another argument with Brownie. The last time he blew his stack completely and slugged poor old Brownie, put a mouse on his cheek bone as big as your fist, almost She had to order Junior out of the house that time because, after all, Brownie hadn't known what he was doing or saying and, besides, one of the Ten Commandments said to honor thy father along with thy mother, didn't it?

Whenever she thought of Brownie and Junior it made her Sad, and when she was sad she had to eat something, so she slipped from beneath the covers, quiet as she could be, and tiptoed across the hotel room to her handbag on the chair near the window. She got the rolls out of her bag, and although the paper napkin she had wrapped them in crackled fit to wake the dead, Elsie Harding didn't stir.

She sat on the edge of the chair in her slip with the pinned shoulder strap (Well, how did I know anybody was going to see it?) and munched her two rolls and thought about Vitto Falconetti and the power she held over That big rich, handsome man and his beautiful wife, whom Lorraine Brown hated.

The second or third day of the trial, somebody bad whispered that there was Mrs. 'Falconetti, the one in the back row in the fur coat, and she had 'finally picked her out, a lovely, pampered woman in a coat that must have been the most expensive anybody could buy, sable, probably or chinchilla. While the Lawyers had talked and talked, she had cast surreptitious glances at Mrs. 'Falconetti, first admiring her, then envying her, and finally hating her for, being so handsome, so immaculate, so rich and poised. She had told herself that there was a woman who had everything—everything—while she, Lorraine Brown, had -nothing, and where was the justice in that? Lorain had always been a decent woman; she went to church regularly, or at least as regularly as she could, Sunday morning usually being an awful rough time for Brownie until one o'clock, when the bars opened. But when she had to stay home to nurse Brownie through the horrors, she usually listened to a church service on the radio and bowed her head when the minister said a prayer, and there used to be plenty of times when she got down on her knees alone to ask God to take the curse of drink oft Brownie, make him listen to the people who tried to get him to go to A.A., either that or carry him off quick, before they had to lock him up in the crazy house.

(And maybe that was why her prayers weren't-answered, that fast. Maybe she'd prayed harder that Brownie would be carried off, put out of his misery, than when she had asked that he be cured. Maybe she'd rather see him dead than have him sober and then worry every minute for fear he'd go back on the sauce)

Anyway, as Lorraine had looked at Mrs. 'Falconetti, the strange hate had grown stronger until the thought had feel the dread that had spread through her like a slowly widening stain.

"Vitto," she faltered, "what's the matter?" But she knew. She knew! And- her first abysmal thought was hate to wrap a package.

Yes, she knew, but she stood there, asking him again' and again what the matter was, until he blurted it out in a gabbling recitation that couldn't have been at all like the statement he must have rehearsed on his way to her, places. And before that, how many times had he silently said the words, told her that he did not love her, that he couldn't deceive her any longer? And always ending' up with the utterly ridiculous statement, "It's bettor you Should find out now than after it's too late

The fool actually believed that she thought it- was better for her to know he didn't love her then, a few days, hours, minutes before the Wedding and what would follow the wedding, than to many her and make her a real woman and never mind what happened after that. Vitto thought he was being honorable, when anyone with half a mind could have seen the honorable thing would be to keep his mouth shut, marry that girl, save her from the humiliation of being jilted no matter if he had to grit his teeth to kiss her at the alter.

If there had been another woman, perhaps she could have forgiven him, but there was no other woman. No, the truth was that Vitto had just gotten scared at the last minute, panic-stricken at the idea of taking on the responsibility of a wife and—and a family. Because there would have been a family, half a dozen adorable children for Elsie to raise as the healthiest, moat polite, model children of the whole neighborhood.

If she hadn't been so totally crushed, if she had, had ....more backbones, she could have argued the point, made Vitto see that this was just a passing aberration or that if it wasn't, plenty of couples got married with one of the other or even both doubting the depth of their love and learning to love each other as they lived together. That was what she should have done, of course, but no, not Elsie Harding; such a thing would have been beneath her, too much like pleading to be taken on any terms. She mouthed some words about yes, it was better that they found out now before it was too late, and she let him. go, good luck, God bless you. Like. the idiot she was, she did not fight to keep the only man who had ever meant a thing to her, the only one who would ever mean a thing to. her.

She knew her friends murmured among themselves that she had handled it very well, in a very civilized way. She wrote correct little notes to everybody concerned, mailed back the lovely presents; found herself a new secretarial job with a firm of architects, although Mr. Kitteridge had begged her to stay on with him, something she couldn't do, not after the way she had lorded it over the other girls, showing them Vitto's ring. She moved to another apartment in another part of the city, where nobody could see her in the delicatessen and whisper to somebody else that there was the girl who had been jilted at the last minute, left standing at the altar, so to speak.

After Vitto, she met dozens of men who wanted to carry the acquaintance further, and they all left her cold. Cold, that was how she felt about almost everything. She read a lot of books that neither stimulated nor bored her, saw a lot of movies and plays that failed to move her, went on vacations to the mountains or the beach and was glad when they were over. She played a technically sound, un-imaginative game of bridge, and this brought her invitations, usually to fill in for a late dropout. She attended a church near her apartment fairly regularly but took no part in its activities apart from its worship services.

Several times after Vitto, men propositioned her, and once when she was walking near her home just after dark a degenerate exposed himself to her, and all these encounters with sex produced the same reaction in her, one of cold repugnance. The idea of an affair interested her not, at all, nor did she encourage any close friendship with another woman. No, she would live out her life without Vitto in the cold semi vacuum in which he had left her when she had finally shut the door on his stammered pleas for forgiveness, that night he had told her that be could not bear the thought of marrying her, after all.

It was only at night, trying to sleep, that the memories, the anticipations, the fears, came free from the confines in which she kept them during the day and rioted through her mind until they were banished by Seconal. And now, unless she wanted to risk an outburst of the Brown woman's empty chatter by going to her bag to get her pillbox, Elsie Harding must lie there and think about this other Vitto, this Vitto 'Falconetti, and wonder if she should vote for him to live or die.

If she voted not guilty, would it be because she had once loved a Vitto and still did, beneath the coldness? If she voted guilty, might it not be because she somehow wanted to punish that other Vitto for what he had done to her, because he had made her this cold, capable, self-contained, utterly useless woman instead of letting her become the wife and mother she had been born to be?

Wouldn't a guilty vote be a reflection of her aversion toward all men since Vitto? On the other hand, might not, a not-guilty ballot be some sort of insincere that she let the catastrophe of nearly seven years ago f rule her still?

She broke off her thoughts as Mrs. Brown came tip-toeing back to the other twin bed. There was the subdued creak of the box spring as the heavy, sagging woman lowered herself into bed. The empty-headed, loose-tongued woman who pinned a broken shoulder strap of her slip rather than bother to sew it, whose skin and hair and nails showed she had quit caring for herself, if she ever had. The unattractive, sloppy, ignorant, opinionated, care-less thinking woman whose son and daughter and invalid husband and two grandchildren (for Lorraine Brown had insisted on telling Elsie all about her family) gave her life a meaning that was denied Elsie Harding, spinster.

CHAPTER EIGHT

In a Cell not far from where Vitto 'Falconetti slept on his cot, Herb Jaffee gave up trying to will sleep his way. He suddenly swung his feet over the edge of the narrow bunk and sat up, then grunted and cursed as his back ' stabbed him with a reminder that it was a mistake to move quickly after lying still so long.

Oh, my aching back was supposed to be a laugh, a gag, but it was no joke to Herb Jaffee. All his life, even when he was a punk kid, he'd had a bad back that nobody believed. Everybody thought he was phutzing off when he had to quit a game or a job or a fight on account of that lousy back, and when he went to the doctors about it they all acted as though he was wasting their time, those that didn't make him spend his dough on corsets and braces and junk that never did him any good. They could talk all they wanted about how medical science had licked about everything there was except cancer, but they still didn't know their tail from a hole in the ground about a bad back, or Herb Jaffee's bad back, anyway. And rather than admit they didn't, they gave him a lot of horse manure about it being all in his head. Psycho-somatic, one doc said, and when Herb asked him what the hell that meant, this wise guy had told him that the subconscious was causing this pain in his back to rationalize his desire to escape the normal competitions of life. Get him! This guy had never had to really work a day in his life, and he was telling a fell who had never had a chance that he was suffering night and day because he didn't want to get in any contests.

That doc was the wig picker at— Well, what difference did it make what prison it was; every stone john had one, and Herb went up in front of them all when he tried to get off heavy work in the shops. Not that it ever did biro any good a session with the head shirker and bang, right back to the rottenest duty in the joint they'd show him what happened to a guy who tried to kiss the dog.

Jaffee thought of the prison he'd probably be going to, when this trial was over (if the crummy D.A.'s office didn't cross him up), and found the prospect dismal. It was better than the chair, but that was all it was better than. The last time Herb had been in that joint they'd a like to killed him with the heavy work they put on him. Oh no, it was never in a way that anybody could squawk to the warden about or get the other cons mad about; they just gave him jobs they knew would bust his back, and when he griped about it the screws and the other cons all told him for crissake, pipe down, didn't he know his act was a flop? If that wasn't enough, they took away his good time, too, claiming he was a malingerer, a quisby.

Nothing but trouble for poor Herb Jaffee, ever since the day he was born. Without that bad back he could have shown em, too. If he wasn't half-crippled where it didn't show, he could have outfoxed the whole stinking world. He had the brains to do it; it was just that a guy couldn't operate

79

right when his back was killing him. That was the reason he took so many falls. That was the reason

And it was a real bad fix and liable to get worse if that jury that was sleeping in those soft hotel beds, not a bad back in the lot, came in with a not-guilty verdict for 'Falconetti. In that case it could very well be the Old Smoky for Herb Jaffee, and with his luck that was probably the way things would turn out.

The way they worked it, when he had offered to white eye, turn People's evidence, they made him a lot of promises without really promising him a damn thing. They told him that if he'd confess to killing that slob, Ferriss, and then testify that Vitto 'Falconetti had arranged the whole deal, they'd "take it into consideration," they'd "see what could be done," they'd "certainly review any recommendations with an eye to his full cooperation in the prosecution of 'Falconetti." And what did that mean if 'Falconetti got off? Not one stinking thing. Not a word down in black and white. Not a single out-and-out promise that they'd go easy on him even if they did give 'Falconetti the complete treatment. And if they missed 'Falconetti, who would they turn on? Herb Jaffee, that's who. With his confession on the record and 'Falconetti cleared of any part of it, what else would they be likely to do, just open the cell door and say thanks for your full cooperation and here's a ticket to China, get lost?

And even if they did that, China wouldn't be far enough away from 'Falconetti if the big boy pulled a not guilty out of the hat. 'Falconetti never forgot, never forgave. Guys that had done a lot less to Vitto 'Falconetti had disappeared and never been heard from again, except by the grapevine that knew what had happened to them, all right.

He wouldn't be safe from 'Falconetti, even in the can, if 'Falconetti got off this hook. The civilians might think that when a man was locked up he was safe from the guys outside who wanted lo see him dead or busied up bad, but the civilians didn't know how far people like Vitto 'Falconetti could reach in the world, had to come in with a guilty verdict. They had to. Hadn't he fingered 'Falconetti hard enough? Hadn't 'Falconetti stayed off the stand, and wouldn't that mean anything to those knot heads? He was afraid to take the stand, you jerks! He might be the biggest, toughest guy in the world, but he was scared that if he took the stand somebody would ask the right question that would show everybody that 'Falconetti had plenty reason to kill his pal, Dan Ferriss, because his wife had been sleeping around with Handsome Dan.

Yeah, he had laid it all out for the D.A., an open and shut case, but that jerk Wolfe had gone for the other angle, the one he'd claimed he had tangible proof of, 'Falconetti's yen to get rid of a business competitor the hard way. The other, the juicier bit that the jury would have eaten up, Wolfe had thrown right out the window, hearsay, inadmissible. Even if true—even if true—the People's case would have to be based on a rather contemptible type of evidence, and the jury would react unfavorably.

Long words right out of the dictionary. These educated basturd's were the worst kind. Wolfe had looked like he was wiser than God when he spilled these big words, wrecking his own case, but it wasn't Wolfe's tit that was in the wringer, it was Herb Jaffee's, the guy that never had a real chance on account of his bad back.

CHAPTER NINE

"Do you want a sleeping pill, dear?" Elizabeth Wolfe asked her husband. "A glass of warm milk?"

"Unh-unh," Charley said. "No, I think I'll go out in the den and sit for a while. I always get sleepy sitting in my chair, no matter how I try to stay bright and witty, so maybe that's the answer."

Beth started to warn her husband not to fall asleep in the chair and wake up all stiff and aching, as he so often did, but she did not speak. Better for Charley to get some sleep sitting up than to spend the whole night without shutting his eyes, and if he woke up stiff she could massage the cramps away. "wrap up good. Don't catch cold."

Wolfe found his robe and slippers and felt his way to the small room where he had earlier watched TV and eaten his sandwiches, drunk his tea. He fell into the old worn chair with a sigh and leaned back his head. Now that it was too late, much too late, he wondered if perhaps he shouldn't have dismissed so hastily Jaffee's first impossible version of the Ferriss killing.

But the man was so obviously a pathological liar, so crude in his whining attempts to prove himself a defender of another men's marriage, an avenger of a wronged husband, that what who could possibly have listened without retching? To crucify a man who was a thousand times as likely to be innocent as guilty on the babblings of a man like Herb Jaffee— no, that wouldn't have been right. More than that (because, let's face it, he had on occasion crucified witnesses, men and women, to get at a guilty defendant), it would not have been good trial strategy to attack 'Falconetti along those lines. Jaffee had not one single shred of proof to back up his claims. He said he bad spied on Dan Ferriss alone with blackmail in mind, and what he said had happened between Ferriss and Mrs. 'Falconetti was supposed to have taken place in Ferriss' apartment. He was supposedly watched from a convenient half-constructed building across the street, with not a hotel-registry entry or a bellboy's recollection to support Jaffee's claim that 'Falconetti had sent him out to kill Ferriss because Handsome Dan was his wife's lover.

No, it would have been a disastrous course to take. Rita Troy and her PI would have made hash of that "evidence," even if Judge Cleveland had allowed it, and between them the Defense would have made the jury so indignant at this base slander against Mrs. 'Falconetti (beautiful but sad, too, and not only because her husband was in trouble) that the jurors wouldn't have had to leave the box to declare 'Falconetti innocent.

Jaffee's second story, the line of attack Wolfe had chosen, was the sounder because Vitto 'Falconetti had obviously started to pull the rug out from under Dan Ferriss, to wreck his business and eliminate him as a competitor. The reason for 'Falconetti's sudden change from friend to enemy was not for the District Attorney's office to guess It was enough that Ferriss was the only man , who ranked close to 'Falconetti in the industry, and that 'Falconetti had set in motion secret machinations that would have bankrupted Ferriss in a year, if Jaffee's bullet had not ended his life first, machinations that could be proved in court with admissible evidence. And if, indeed, 'Falconetti had hired Jaffee to kill Ferriss, it could very well have been because of some deadly surge of rage that made the other course of destruction too slow, too impersonal, not decisive enough to satisfy 'Falconetti.

Wolfe envisioned 'Falconetti's square, handsome face as he had first seen it and wondered again whether he was one of the greatest actors who had ever lived or if he actually did feel so superior to the situation that he could look and talk as he had.

Hardly had he been let into the office before he said, in that hard, bitter voice of his, "Let me say it before you do. You're an Assistant District Attorney and you're going to ask me some questions and I don't have to answer them."

Charley, sitting at his desk, had been able to do nothing more than look up at this big man, almost dropping his jaw in his surprise. He had expected a goon in expensive clothing; Vitto 'Falconetti looked more like a onetime Ivy League fullback who had kept himself in shape even though the banking business he had inherited had interfered with his polo and ocean racing.

"But if I do answer your questions," 'Falconetti was saying, "anything I say may be used against me. Well, friend, I'll answer any question you have to ask, so you go right ahead and indulge yourself."

"That's very kind of you, Mr. 'Falconetti," was Charley's rejoinder.

The wide mouth stretched in a smile that bore more than a trace of contempt. "I've always been known as a kind man," 'Falconetti said. "Ten years ago I won the kindest-man award at the annual bricklayers' ball. So suppose yon start asking your questions."

"All right," Wolfe said. "Did you contract to have Daniel Ferriss murdered?"

"No."

"Do you know a man named Herbert Jaffee?"

"No."

"Did you give Herbert Jaffee one thousand dollars to kill Daniel Ferriss?"

"No."

"Did you know Daniel Ferriss?"

"Yes."

"How did you know him?"

"He was in the same business I'm in, bricks," Vitto said.

Wolfe asked, "He owned a firm that competed with yours?"

The big man who stood before Charley's desk hunched his shoulders slightly. "I couldn't handle the whole market. I will someday but not yet. Dan's company is the next biggest. I suppose you could call him a competitor. We bid on the same jobs, most of them."

"But wasn't his competition hurting your business pretty badly lately?" Charley watched 'Falconetti closely, but there was no telltale flicker of a sign.

"I just said we bid on the same jobs. When Dan got the contract and I didn't, I suppose you could call it hurting my business. And by the way you asked that question, I guess somebody gave you the scoop on the Quigley Building deal. Yes, I could say that hurt me. I'd counted on getting that bid."

Wolfe paused, and then asked, "With Ferriss dead, what happens to the Quigley job? Will his company continue to operate, Mr. 'Falconetti?"

"You tell me, Mr. D.A.," 'Falconetti said evenly. "I don't know how Dan left his affairs or who he's got who could step in and take over. Dan Ferriss and I were pretty good friends, but not to the point where he told me how he was running his business any more than I told him how I was running mine.

Charley shuffled some papers on his desk, inspecting one carefully and hesitating over it before putting it on the bottom of the stack. Finally he asked, "You say you were pretty good friends. Does that mean you traveled together socially, outside of business circles, Mr. 'Falconetti?"

The other man gave a short, toneless laugh. "Your office hasn't given you much of a line on me, has it?" he asked. "Because if yon know anything about me you know I don't have any social life. I'm strictly business. I leave the social bit up to Mrs. 'Falconetti."

And then, for that moment, Wolfe was tempted to dig a little deeper into the possibilities of Jaffee's first story. "Did Mrs. 'Falconetti and Ferriss travel in the same social circles, then, or was Ferriss as strictly business as you?" There was no change in 'Falconetti's expression, no change in his voice. "Yeah, Dan and my wife went places together, if that's what you mean. He was a bachelor and he liked to go to the same places she did, he seemed to be able to afford to waste time like that, so they went places and did things together."

"I see," Charley Wolfe said. "And this, of course, was perfectly all right with you."

Vitto 'Falconetti's gray-green eyes held Wolfe's as they deepened with what might have been derision. "Look, Mr. D.A.," the big man said, "Lou and Dan Ferriss have been seen together all around San Francisco for the past three or four years. If it hadn't been perfectly all right with me, they wouldn't have gone out once together."

He looked at the girl taking down this conversation on her Stenotype, then half-turned to glance back at the two witnesses in the officer, the policeman near the door and the law clerk, was were there in case anything said here had to be corroborated m court, and finally looked back at Charley Wolfe.

"I guess I see what you're getting at," he said, "but if you think I killed Dan Ferriss or had him killed because I thought there was anything wrong between him and my wife, you don't know me, you don't know Mrs. 'Falconetti, and you don't know what Dan was like, either." Again that matter-of-fact tone, the utter absence of fear or anger or even emphasis, employed to drive home a point. It was uncanny. This man 'Falconetti was unique in Wolfe's long experience.

Trying to get back command of this interview, Charley asked, "I see—then you had Daniel Ferriss killed for strictly business reasons, is that it?"

"No," 'Falconetti replied patiently. "No, I didn't have him killed at all." He paused and then he said, "Now let me ask one question. Are all the people in the D.A.'s office as stupid as yon are?"

The insult caught Wolfe by surprise, knocking him off balance. He felt his face flush as the anger flared through him and a hot rejoinder leaped up into his month, something senseless like a threat, or an obscenity, but he kept : control and only jerked his head toward the policeman standing by the door to the adjoining office. "Bring him in, please," he said, and his voice was remarkably even, almost as though 'Falconetti had not delivered his remark at all.

'Falconetti looked at Charley keenly and asked, "Is it all right for me to smoke or is it against the rules?"

"Go ahead," Wolfe said, and watched the big man, deliberately turn his back on the door through which the cop was leading Herb Jaffee; the People's witness whose testimony could send him to the Gas Chamber.

Although Wolfe had rejoiced at Jaffee's confession and his willingness to turn State's evidence as a break; that might finally bring overdue Justice to a ruthless man who, had gotten away with coercion, intimidation, mayhem, and probably murder in his headlong career. He had always wished that Jaffee were not the specimen he actually was, weak-chinned, with little ferret's eyes that could never meet another's squarely. Jaffee had a long record of arrests, most of them for crimes that had not required courage or even recklessness, such as peeping Tom, petit larceny, attempted extortion, contributing to the delinquency of a minor, the shabby little offenses done by shabby little misfits. And this man was supposed to have murdered Handsome Dan Ferriss; this weakling. Herb Jaffee, was supposed to have been hired by a powerhouse like Vitto 'Falconetti to kill a business (or love) rival? It had seemed incredible at first, but there was Jaffee's confession, backed up by police evidence, and Jaffee had named 'Falconetti as his employer, and Wolfe's superiors had told him to shoot with the ammunition he had.

"The biggest, smartest ones sometimes get feeling so secure that they make stupid mistakes," the big boss had told Charley. "Proceed on the assumption that Vitto 'Falconetti considers himself bigger than the law and slipped up this one time,"

As Jaffee came toward Wolfe's desk, 'Falconetti made a production of lighting his cigarette, the first unnatural move. be had made since entering the office. Long after the tobacco had caught, 'Falconetti kept the lighter to it, puffing clouds of smoke, keeping his back firmly turned to Jaffee, and this one move gave Wolfe his first thrill of hope that the big man could be had, that his shell might not be quite so invulnerable as it had first seemed.

Jaffee came up beside 'Falconetti, peered at the taller man, gulped, and said, "Hello, Mr. 'Falconetti."

'Falconetti snapped his lighter shut, then looked at Jaffee. The eyes and voice he turned on Wolfe dripped scorn. "No," he said. "This proves you've got to be the stupidest one of the bunch, Wolfe."

Charley was able to smile back. "Maybe," he said, before he turned to Jaffee and asked, "Mr. Jaffee, who is this man?"

"Vitto 'Falconetti," Jaffee said, and gulped again.

"And what can you tell me about him?" Charley asked.

"He paid me a thousand dollars to kill Dan Ferriss," Jaffee recited. "I didn't want to but he made me."

"He paid you in cash?" Wolfe asked.

"Yeah, five hundred down and five hundred when I did the job."

"Did he hand you the money personally?"

"Uh-huh. I mean, yes, he did," Jaffee said.

Wolfe turned to 'Falconetti then and found the scorn still present in the big man's eyes, deeper, if anything. "Is there anything you want to say about that, Mr. 'Falconetti?" he asked.

The big multimillionaire leaned over to tap the ash from his cigarette in a tray. "Oh, boy," he said softly, almost to himself. "This is one for the book, this is. Is there anything I want to say, the man asks me." He straightened, and his eyes bored into Wolfe's. "Okay, Mr. District Attorney, you're making a problem for me. And if you know anything at all about me, you know that's a ridiculous kind of thing to do to Vitto Falconetti. You keep on and you're going to wind up being hurt, little man, hurt bad."

Despite himself, Charley Wolfe felt a twinge of fear even as he thrust out his chin and asked stiffly, "Are you threatening me, Mr. 'Falconetti?"

'Falconetti waited a moment before he asked deliberately, "Have you got any good reason why I shouldn't threaten you, beefer?"

Later, when 'Falconetti had been booked murder-one and was on his way to the County Jail, Wolfe asked an old-timer connected with the D-A's office just what "beefer" meant.

"It means prosecutor, especially a D.A.," the retired policeman explained. "Haven't heard the word in years, it's strictly east coast, like 'have you got a beef or problem' or 'What's you beef' with me. You must have got hold of an old hood there, Mr. Wolfe."

"No," Charley replied," or at least I don't think so.

Vitto 'Falconetti just called me 'beefer.'"

"'Falconetti? huh, he must've run with the boys back during Prohibition, but he sure don't look like it, does he? I saw him when they were taking him away, and he looked as though he was inspecting the place with an idea of buying it. Plenty of brass, you got to give him that."

"Mm-hm," Charley agreed, nodding slowly, "and any time a man is that sure of himself, no matter what he's done, I worry."

The old-timer said sagely, "With him, you've got reason to worry. You take all the things he's got away with since he first come up and they'd reach from here to the moon and back."

"This one he's not going to get away with," Wolfe said firmly.

But now, sitting in his den, the low-set thermostat letting a chill creep into him, the jury locked up for the night and thinking or dreaming only God knew what, he was dismally sure that the murder of Dan Ferriss had a good chance of becoming just another addition to that string of unpunished crimes that reached to the moon and back.

CHAPTER TEN

Room 232 of the Hotel Inness was finally quiet, both its occupants, Anson Benedict and Charles Williams, silenced at last, their furious loud voice argument stilled by sheer need for sleep, not by any change in stubborn conviction.

Anson Benedict was Juror Number 12, Williams was Number 11, and of all the jurors who had been lodged in the Inness for the night, these two most flagrantly broke that unenforceable rule against discussing the case. Williams, a middle-aged (fifty-five) service-station owner, thought the rule was crazy to begin with; in the second place, he regarded it as his bounden duty as a citizen, veteran, and straight thinker to set this young (thirty-eight) Benedict guy right for keeps when he got him alone, with no foreman to bust into his argument with any complaints about him monopolizing the floor and being too loud besides.

Benedict's stand was identical, in reverse.

The pair had struck sparks from the beginning, and for no other reason except that they were two of a kind. Each man was argumentative, hardheaded, and convinced that he and he alone had absorbed alt the testimony, weighed it judiciously, and reached an infallibly just decision based solely on evidence and due process of the law without a trace of personal prejudice. That they had reached opposite conclusions was perhaps inevitable, and the debate between them had been going on ever since each had found the other on the wrong side of the fence.

Neither had bothered to examine the motives behind the immediate antagonism that had raised itself between them, and when this case was finished each would go his separate way with no more thought of the other than an occasional reference to that know-it-all sonofabitch who had made things tough on everybody by refusing to admit he was as wrong as a three dollar bill. The fact was, as could have been pinpointed by some omniscient presence (or perhaps by a computer), that Williams and Benedict were parallel personalities, separated by some seventeen years. They constituted a phenomenon that was fated never to be recognized, two men whose lives had followed and would continue to follow eerily similar paths.

The older juror, Charles Williams, was born in New Britain, Connecticut, on August 20, 1920. Anson Benedict was born in Holyoke, Massachusetts, on (get this!) August 20, 1937. Both finished their education when they graduated from their respective high schools, in which each had been a B-minus student and had played football and baseball. Both men went into factories immediately upon leaving high school, Williams into a hardware plant and Benedict into a textile mill. Each married at the age of twenty-three, and each produced a son in the second year of marriage, a daughter in the fourth, and another daughter in the seventh. Both men came to California at the urging of relatives (in Benedict's case a brother-in-law, an uncle in Williams') who were startling businesses that subsequently failed, bringing on hard times for about eighteen months until each made a good connection in his present line of work, a gas station in Williams' case and a chain shoe store in Benedicts

Each man served in World War II. Despite his thirty-three years, Williams found himself in the infantry and was wounded by a grenade in August, 1944, in the diversionary invasion of the south of France, a sideshow attraction known as Operation Dragoon.

Benedict was also an infantryman and was wounded in France the day after Williams, got his, although some distance away, at a place called Maceio, where he was fighting with Patton's Third Army. Neither of the wounds was too serious, but they were enough to get both men back: to the States before V-E Day. After that, both Williams and Benedict were active in their separate veterans' organizations, and each hoped someday to be a big wheel therein, even National Commander.

And why did not this amazing series of coincidences —if they could be called that—cement a bond between these two men? Why didn't they find a common interest. In their war experiences, at least, if nothing else? Well, each of them had been wearing a lapel pin denoting his veteran's affiliation when they had first met in the central jury room, before they had been told to take them off, and at the time the two particular groups had been at each other's throat over something to do with one organization's charge that the other's fund-raising direct-mail campaign was a racket. Ergo, Williams and Benedict had their close association since had done nothing to endear one to the other.

It was long after midnight when Williams said, "Okay, okay, let me try to convince you again."

"What do you mean, you convince me?" Benedict replied. "I'm the one that's trying to show you where you're wrong, remember?"

"I've been listening to you sound off ever since this trial started," the older man said icily, "and you don't make sense. Reasonable doubt, man, reasonable doubt! That's the whole thing in a nutshell."

"Nutshell is right. Nutshells to the nuts, I always say."

"No, listen. Didn't the Judge say we've got lo find "'Falconetti guilty beyond a reasonable doubt or he's innocent? Didn't he?"

"Don't tell me what the judge said; I was right there and I heard—"

"Listen. Please, for once in your life listen instead of trying to hog the floor. Okay, so you admit there can't be any reasonable doubt. And there's plenty of reasonable doubt that Vitto 'Falconetti did it, and if you don't see it, then you're soft in the head."

"Look, don't go calling names or I might forget you're older than god and let you have one," Benedict warned.

"That would be fine, wouldn't it?" Williams jeered. "One juror couldn't listen to reason so he had to get sore and plow the guy that was trying to explain things to him. But don't let my age stop you, if that's what you're worrying about."

"Never mind," Benedict said darkly. "Just quit bugging me, that's all."

"I'm not bugging you; I'm trying to make you listen to reason," Williams cried. "Look, I'll prove it to you, about the reasonable doubt, I mean. You sat there and heard just what I heard. All you have to do is think back and remember what you heard. I mean, take Rita Troyer's opening statement Just that alone."

"Ladies and gentlemen of the jury," Rita Troyer had said, "We intend to produce testimony that ought to convince you that you're sitting here in judgment on a crime that has no relationship to the defendant." she paced up and down in front of the jury, slowly, relaxed, purposeful but never dramatic, her occasional hand motions no more than conversational gestures.

"We'll show that the District Attorney has no proof that Vitto 'Falconetti was connected with the crime with which he is charged," she said. "We'll show that the entire case for the State is based on the false testimony of a convicted extortionist, forger, embezzler, and petty thief, a man whose entire adult life has been spent in crime.

"We'll prove that this man, Herbert Jaffee, has sought and obtained special treatment from the District Attorney's office in return for his statement implicating Vitto 'Falconetti in the murder for which 'Falconetti is being tried. We'll show that this man, Jaffee, who attempts to excuse himself of the crime of murder by claiming merely to have been an unwilling hired hand, is in reality the man who conceived of and committed this crime. And finally we'll point out the strange and questionable logic of the District Attorney's : office, which asks the death sentence for the man they say hired the killer to do his deadly work, but will ask a much lesser sentence for the man who actually put a gun to Daniel Ferriss' head and pulled the trigger." She paused, smiled at the eight men and four women, and completed his opening address with the simple statement, "We expect that you will find reasonable doubt and that you will declare Vitto 'Falconetti not guilty."

"An opening statement," Anson Benedict scoffed. "For God's sake, what did you expect Troyer, to say, that he was licked before she started? She's got to earn his fee, hasn't she? She had to make it sound good to 'Falconetti so it would look like he was getting his money's worth, didn't he?"

"Ahhh, you're hopeless," Williams grunted. "All during the trial you looked like you had your mind made up even before you heard any testimony at all."

"You're the one that had your mind made up," Benedict countered. "Otherwise you wouldn't be giving me all this reasonable-doubt crap. Answer me one question. Just one. 'Falconetti claimed he didn't even know Jaffee. Well, if that's true, then how could Jaffee pick him out of eight million people as the guy who hired him to knock Ferriss off?

"Easy. Jaffee is a—"

"And how did Jaffee even know that 'Falconetti knew Ferriss, huh? How did he know 'Falconetti had a motive to kill him, getting rid of the only guy that kept him from having full control of the racket, the business? You explain that and maybe I'll say okay, there's reasonable doubt." Williams had risen to the challenge eagerly.

"Okay, I will. So maybe 'Falconetti lied at first when he said he didn't know Jaffee. So okay, he told a little lie to protect himself, maybe. But that's not the point. The point is that they never proved 'Falconetti paid him to murder Ferriss. Why should he? He was after Ferriss' ass, sure, and the D.A. showed how he'd started to put the hooks to Ferriss' business. But if you can ruin a guy in business as easy as 'Falconetti could, louse up Ferriss with strikes and truck breakdowns and stuff like that, why do you knock him off or hire anybody to knock him off? It don't make sense. You want to believe Jaffee's story, it's your privilege. Go ahead and let that small-time hood make a monkey out of you with his fairy tales."

"Fairy tales?" Benedict asked. "It sounded all right to me and at least he got on the stand, which is more than your great Vitto 'Falconetti had guts enough to do."

"Yeah, he got on the stand, all right. He said everything the D.A. coached him to say, that's what Jaffee did."

After Charley Wolfe had asked Herb Jaffee his name and his age, he asked, "For how long have you known the defendant?"

"Vitto 'Falconetti? About a year and a half, close to two years," Jaffee said. His voice was clear and strong. Being on the witness stand, having everybody looking at him and straining to catch every word he said, had always given him a big charge, even when everything ended, with him going down the sewer pipe again.

"How did you meet him?" Wolfe asked.

"I worked for him. Well, not for him personally, you understand. I got a job with a company that he owns, along with half a dozen other—"

"Never mind that," Wolfe interrupted. "What kind of job was this?"

"I was a bricklayer."

"And the name of the company?"

"Falconetti Brickwork, Incorporated. I got steered to this place by a friend of mine. He said it was one of Falconetti's companies and 'Falconetti was probably the only one that could fix it with the union for me to get a job." Tracy felt, rather than heard, Rita Troyer start to get to her feet with an objection about this hearsay testimony concerning Vitto 'Falconetti's ability to "fix it with the union" and went on hastily. "Tell me, Mr. Jaffee," he said, "did you see Mr. 'Falconetti regularly while you worked for Falconetti Brickwork?"

The witness hunched his narrow shoulders. "He came around to look over the job every once in a while, maybe once a week, every ten days, like that."

"Did Mr. 'Falconetti know you?" the Assistant District Attorney asked. "Know you by name, I mean?"

"Sure," Jaffee said readily. "You ask anybody in brickwork and they'll tell you Vitto 'Falconetti knows everybody by name. He makes it his business to. He always called me Herbie."

Wolfe heard a stifled grunt that came from the direction. of the defense table. Judge Cleveland's gavel tapped once, a warning to 'Falconetti to suppress any further audible reactions to the testimony. He then cautioned Jaffee not to volunteer information.

"Now, Mr. Jaffee," Wolfe went on, "did something take place during the week of February 26, 1964?"

"Uh-huh. I mean, yes, sir. Mr. 'Falconetti had a conversation with me.

"Where did this conversation take place, and what, in words or substance, did each of you say?"

Herb's back was doing fine, not a twinge. He spoke slowly, like the stinking D.A. had told him to. "Right. Well, I was working on a scaffold on this apartment house. We're up about twelve stories, and it was a Friday around three o'clock, windy, and I'm freezing my—"

He broke oft as a ripple of courtroom laughter, the most easily triggered anywhere on the face of the earth, ran its course. The judge tapped his gavel again and the room was still.

"So Mr. 'Falconetti gets on the scaffold with me and sends my partner away," Jaffee went on. "He says he wants to talk to me. Okay, so he's the big wheel, so I got to listen. And I mean he comes right to the point. He don't fool around. He says he'll give me a thousand dollars cash, five hundred now and five hundred after, if I kill this guy Dan Ferriss for him."

He paused and looked at Vitto 'Falconetti, meeting the big man's eyes squarely and saying silently, Okay, you rich bastard, suffer a little like I always have.

The D.A.'s voice brought him back to the task at hand. "Go on," Charles Wolfe said.

"So I told him I couldn't do nothing like that," Jaffee said. "He said I'd better do what he said or maybe I'd have a scaffold rope break on me or something. He could do it, too. So I said I'd think it over. He said let him know Monday. He said he had a gun for me and he'd finger this guy Ferriss for me."

"Finger?" Wolfe asked.

"Point him out, finger him. He said he'd be around Monday and the answer had better be yes and don't try to leave town or anything because it wouldn't be no use, he'd find me."

"And did he see you the following Monday?"

"Yes. He was there early Monday morning and I told him I'd do it. I was too scared of him to say anything else and he knew it."

The judge, anticipating Troyer's objection, ordered the last sentence stricken and instructed the jury to disregard it.

"What happened then?"

"He gave me five bills and the gun."

At that point Wolfe went to a table, picked up a gun, and brought it back toward the witness stand. "I show you this object and I ask if you identify it." Herb made a big thing out of examining the heater.

When he handed it back to Wolfe he nodded and said, "That's the gun he gave me."

"I offer it in evidence." Wolfe said, handing it to the court officer, "as People's Exhibit Number One. And what, if anything, did you do with this gun?"

"Well, the next Saturday night I shot this guy Ferriss through the head with it and dumped him out of the car in a vacant lot on East Houston Street," Jaffee recited. "I ditched the car uptown and went home."

"What happened after that?"

"Well, Mr. 'Falconetti gave me the rest of the thousand bucks, the other five hundred. He told me I did a good Job and he might have some more work for me."

Wolfe picked up the automatic. "Did he say anything to you in connection with this gun?" he asked,

"Yeah, when he gave it to me he told me to get rid of it after I used it," Jaffee replied.

"When he paid me off. I told him I threw it in the ocean."

"Did you?"

"No, I kept it."

"Did you have any reason for doing that, Mr. Jaffee?"

Herb hesitated, then shook his head as the enormity of his own stupidity overwhelmed him. If he hadn't kept the damned gun, nobody would have ever been able to lean on him for this job, not in a hundred million years. Who did he think he was, a tough hood or somebody? What did he need with a gun after he glommed Ferriss? But it was worth dough, real nice dough, after it cooled off, and so he had hidden it in a bureau drawer (some hiding place!), and when some rat-fink tipped off the cops they came right to his place and it took them about five seconds to come up with the gun.

"Mr. Jaffee?" Wolfe was prompting.

"No," Jaffee said sullenly. "I don't know. I just kept It. that's all I got this bad back and when it hurts me I don't think straight I get mixed up and—"

"That' all Mr. Jaffee" Wolfe cut in. "Your witness, Ms. Troyer."

CHAPTER ELEVEN

In Room 228 of the Inness, Jurors Seven and Eight, Louis Kobel and John Gier, slept soundly, their minds made up, no room for argument or self-searching. Both jurors had voted not guilty on the first ballot and had stuck to it through the subsequent polls; in the morning they would go back to the jury room and keep on voting not guilty.

Yes, they both admitted, Vitto 'Falconetti must have lied at the start when he told the D.A. he didn't know Herb Jaffee, and yes, the D.A. had brought up some pretty strong evidence that 'Falconetti had started in motion some undercover work that was aimed at killing his supposed best friend, Dan Ferriss; both Gier and Kobel could admit that, but the fact still remained that they could place no faith in the testimony of the People's star witness, Jaffee, and without his story, there was plenty of reasonable doubt for both jurors, with some left over.

Just think of the way the defense counsel, Rita Troyer, had ripped Jaffee apart, chewed him up in little pieces. According to Kobel and Gier's way of thinking, no juror in his right mind could give Jaffee's testimony that much weight after Troyer had gotten through with him.

The mild way Troyer had started off hadn't given the jury any sign of the savage attack that was coming. Smiling, friendly, the defense attorney had approached the witness stand where Jaffee sat waiting, moistening his lips now and then in his nervousness, and the lawyer's voice had been almost gentle.

"Well, Mr. Jaffee, that was quite a story you just gave the jury," Rita said. "Believe me, all of us here in the courtroom listened carefully to everything you said. Everything."

"Well, it's the truth," Jaffee said, still sullen, his back beginning the dull ache; that was always the preliminary to the real bad time.

"Now, thinking back over it carefully, Mr. Jaffee, wouldn't you say that" and Rita's voice changed, took on a bite, hammered at the unprepared witness with an impact that made Jaffee rear back in his chair— "wouldn't you say that you fabricated the entire story? That none of it actually happened? Isn't that true, Mr. Jaffee?"

"No," Jaffee cried. "I tell you it happened."

"It did, eh?" Rita calmed her voice as her manner became brittle, matter-of-fact. "Well, then, let's go into this story of yours, bit by bit. You say you were hired as a bricklayer by Vitto 'Falconetti and—"

"No," Jaffee broke in. "I didn't say that. I said I hired on with a company that everybody knows 'Falconetti owns even if it's supposed to be somebody else's. That's what I said."

"Oh?" Rita seemed genuinely surprised at the different version. "Do you mean you're acquainted with the financial and corporate structure of this company? Do you have information that this company has an interlocking directorate with Mr. 'Falconetti's corporation, 'Falconetti Builders Supply? Perhaps you can explain how you—"

"I didn't say I knew; I said everybody knows," Jaffee interrupted.

"Does that mean everybody knows but you?" Rita asked. "I'm confused, Mr. Jaffee. Suppose you tell us again how you know that this company you were employed by, 'Falconetti Brickwork, was actually controlled by-"

"Your Honor," Charley Wolfe said "I object to the form of the question, and to the whole line of questioning, as argumentative."

"I'm merely trying to establish the acumen and veracity of the State's own. witness," Rita argued. "The witness has made a statement, and I merely want him to elucidate a bit for the benefit of the jury, to prove or disprove the fact that as a witness under oath he has been testifying to facts he can verify. Surely this is—"

"All right, Ms. Troyer," Judge Cleveland said dryly. "Let's proceed from the fact that this witness claims to have worked for 'Falconetti Brickwork, regardless of its ownership, corporate structure, interlocking directorates, and so on."

"Yes, sir," Rita said equably as she nodded off Jaffee, she asked, "You were employed as a bricklayer? Do I have that right, or do you want to correct me there, too?"

"That's right," Jaffee grumbled.

"Where had you worked just previous to that job?" Troyer asked.

"Nowhere." The word was little more than a whisper.

"Nowhere?" Rita asked loudly, surprised again. "Explain that, please."

Jaffee hesitated and then mumbled, "I was in prison." And added under his breath, You knew that, ya crumb.

"In prison?" There seemed to be no end of surprises for Rita Troyer in this witness's testimony. "Could you tell the court and jury the nature of the crime for which you were convicted?"

Jaffee's eyes switched toward Wolfe at the prosecution table. Wasn't the crummy D.A. supposed to object? He'd served his time, every stinking minute of it, so why drag it all out here? But Wolfe was looking down at a pad on the table in front of him, and he didn't seem about to stir.

"Extortion," Jaffee muttered.

"Extortion," Rita repeated, loud and clear. "Had you ever been in prison before that?"

Jaffee cast another glance at Wolfe. No hope. "Yes," he said in a low voice. "For forgery?" All right, spread out the whole stinking jacket, all of it. And let everybody have a good laugh when he told them it was on account of his bad back. "Yes," he said bitterly.

"And is it true that you have been convicted on other occasions of various crimes in other parts of the country, besides those offenses for which you were put on probation?" Rita asked. "And that these crimes date back to your earliest years?"

"Yeah," Herb Jaffee said wearily. "I suppose so."

Rita nodded, half-turned away, and asked over her shoulder, "Now tell me, Mr. Jaffee, did you discuss this case with the District Attorney before he called you to testify?"

"You confessed to killing Daniel Ferriss?" The words were level, knife-edged. "well—yeah. Yes, I did."

"With premeditation?"

What was the use in looking at the D.A.? The sonofabitch must have gone to sleep. "Yes."

"In other words," Rita asked, "you confessed to murder in the first degree?"

"Yes." Herb Jaffee found his throat had suddenly gone dry, and he swallowed hard.

Troyer turned and shot her next question. "Tell me, do you except to be tried for first-degree murder?"

"Huh?" Herb asked, jolted. "What do you mean? I dunno."

Rita bore in. "Mr. Jaffee," she barked, "isn't it true that you were offered a deal by the District Attorney if you agreed to testify in this trial?"

Wolfe was on his feet. "Objection!" he cried. "Isn't that why you confessed?" Troyer asked Jaffee.

"I object, Your Honor," Wolfe shouted. "This is an improper line of questioning, intended to impugn—"

"Overruled," Judge Harrison Cleveland put in. He was a cavernous, brooding-browed man whose appearance belied the immense enjoyment he got out of life, day by day. "I'm going to allow this line of questioning, Mr. Wolfe, on the issue of credibility."

Wolfe seemed about to add another protest, apparently changed his mind, and sank back into his chair. Troyer came closer to the witness stand, pounding home her question-statements now. "Didn't you confess to this murder, Mr. Jaffee, because the District Attorney agreed to allow you to plead guilty to a lesser charge than first degree murder? And didn't lie agree to hold off your trial till the conclusion of this one?"

"No," Jaffee bleated. "He didn't agree to nothing."

"Didn't he say that he would delay your trial, and if your testimony was as you had promised, he would get you some consideration?"

"No, he didn't say anything like that—"

"You haven't been brought to trial yet, have you, Mr. Jaffee?"

"No."

"Your lawyer hasn't asked for any delay or postponement, has he, as far as you know?"

"No, not as far as I know."

"You don't expect to be tried before this trial is over, do you?"

"No."

"Didn't you agree to testify against the defendant in order to save your own life?"

"No," Jaffee said. His voice was dead now. The lousy D.A. had screwed him again. All those promises, and when he finally got off his ass to object, the lousy judge told him to shut up and sit down.. Some D.A. he was.

"Then," Rita was asking him, "give the court and jury the reason why you confessed."

Jaffee's back ached fiercely as it always did when he was confused and frightened. "I don't know," he managed. "I mean, I confessed because I was caught. What I mean, they caught me. I didn't have nothing else to do, did I? They had me by—well, they grabbed me good."

Troyer asked, "Do you know what reason they had for picking you up?"

Jaffee shook his head. "They said it was on account of some pawn ticket, but if you ask me, some fink squealed on me." A great light dawned, and he added "Probably 'Falconetti himself, for all I know."

Troyer shook her head, her half-smile returning. "You know, don't you, that the police witnesses testified that they were investigating the pawning of a stolen camera, and their investigation led them to you. And according to the policemen, when they examined your room they found the gun you used to murder Daniel Ferriss."

"That's what they say," Jaffee mumbled.

"But you testified yourself that they did enter your room and they did find the gun and you were there, is that right?"

"I suppose so."

"What did you tell the police when they questioned you about the gun?" Troyer asked.

"Nothing," Jaffee retorted.

"But what did you tell the District Attorney when he questioned you?" Rita pursued. As Jaffe shut his lizard's mouth more tightly, the defense attorney asked, "Didn't you, and then tell the District Attorney the story you've just told us here?"

"All right," Jaffee burst out. "Maybe I did. So what?" Troyer again half-turned from the witness stand and asked, almost idly, "Tel] me, Mr. Jaffee, how much money did Dan Ferriss have in his pocket when you murdered him?"

"I don't know," Herb said stonily. "You mean you didn't look?"

104

"No, I didn't look."

"Weren't you alone with him in his car?" "Yes."

"Well, how could you pass up a golden opportunity like that?" the defense attorney asked incredulously. "Mr. Ferris was a wealthy man, supposedly carrying quite a lot of money on his person, and yet you say you didn't go throng his pockets? How do you explain that?" Herb hunched his shoulders. I dunno," he said feebly.

"Incidentally, how did you get into Mr. Ferriss' car?" Rita asked curiously.

"Well, I-—well, after 'Falconetti fingered the guy for me, I—-well, I caught up with him at a red light in the heavy cross-town traffic and I just opened the door and got in. I put the gun on him. and told him if he behaved he'd be all right but if he squeaked he was like dead. It was easy."

"Then you had him drive to East Houston Street and there you shot him through the head and dumped him out? Is that right?"

"Yeah, that's right. That's how it happened."

"I see." Rita Troyer paused a long moment to give the Jury a chance to visualize the killing before she asked, "Mr. Jaffee, you heard the testimony of the police officer who discovered Ferris's body, didn't you?"

"Yeah."

"You heard him say that Daniel Ferriss had no money—as a matter of fact, he had no wallet on his person, didn't you?"

"Yeah, I heard," Jaffee grumbled.

"Didn't you steal his wallet?" Troyer asked quietly.

"No! No, I didn't!"

"Isn't that why you killed him?"

"No, I tell you."

"Wasn't it a plain, ordinary mugging?"

"No!" Herb's cry was a forlorn wail.

"And didn't Mr. Ferriss resist and—"

"I said no! Don't you get me? No!"

Rita exchanged her vindictive expression for a more gentle one. "All right, Mr. Jaffee," she said. "Tell me this; did you know, of your own knowledge, that Vitto 'Falconetti and Daniel Ferriss, the man you murdered, were business competitors?"

"Sure, I knew it. Anybody in the business would know that, even a poor slob of a bricklayer trying to get along."

"And didn't it occur to you when the District Attorney was questioning you that you could save your own life by accusing Vitto 'Falconetti of masterminding this killing?"

"No," Jaffee said, his voice husky.

"No, what I said was the truth."

"Who suggested the idea that you testify for the prosecution?" Rita asked. "You or the District Attorney?"

Jaffee shifted in his chair, but it did nothing to ease the pain of his bad back. "He did," he said, after a long hesitation.

"After you concocted the story about Vitto 'Falconetti?" The question was asked easily, almost negligently. "I tell you I didn't concoct it," Jaffee cried.

"But the District Attorney did suggest that you confess and testify, didn't he?" Jaffee's yes dragged out of him reluctantly.

"And didn't he offer you a deal?" Rita asked. When Jaffee closed his thin lips tight again, Troyer asked, "Didn't he say he'd try to go easy on you if you'd help?"

Again Jaffee refused to answer, and Rita asked, "If he didn't, could you tell me why you're helping him?" No answer.

Patiently, Troyer asked, "He did offer you a deal, didn't he, Mr. Jaffee?"

Well, what was the use of stalling any longer? The lousy D.A. just sat there and the judge wouldn't let him talk when he tried to and everybody in this courtroom and the world was against poor Herb Jaffee, so why not talk? "Yes," be mumbled.

"I don't think the jury heard yon.," Rita said.

"Yes! Is that loud enough?"

"Quite loud enough, thank you," Rita Troyer said with a nod. His mouth slanted as she said, "No further questions for this witness Your Honor."

CHAPTER TWELVE

In Room 230 of the Inness, Ann Alspach and Mrs. Vida Cannon were awake at three-fifteen that morning. It was Aim's fault and she was awfully sorry, but she had these nightmares every once in a while when she was overtired and she must have frightened Mrs. Cannon terribly, hadn't she when she started moaning and hollering like that?

It scared me half to death, honey," Mrs. Cannon admitted, "but don't let it bother you. Soon as I got my bearings and put on the light, I saw you were having a bad dream so I woke you up."

"But I've ruined your night's sleep," Aim mourned.

"Look, I'll be asleep a long time when they bury me," Mrs. Cannon said philosophically. "Besides, I can drop off, like, any time I want to. Don't tell anybody but when it got too tiresome back there in the courtroom I Just dropped off. Nobody noticed it, I bet You didn't notice it, did you?"

"You mean you can take a nap with your eyes open?" Aim marveled.

"It's a gift," Mrs. Cannon said modestly. "I've always been able to. In school I was asleep half the time and the teacher never found out." She laughed. "That's why I'm such a dumbbell now, I guess."

"You're no dumbbell," Ann protested. "I think you're the smartest one on the jury, the questions you raised while we were talking over the case between votes."

"Questions I can raise but do I change any of those people's minds?" the older woman asked. "No. Six to six., and tomorrow I bet it's going to be the same way."

When Ann offered her a cigarette from the pack the girl kept beside her on the night table, Mrs. Cannon shook her head. "No, thanks. I don't smoke or drink or run around." She laughed again.

"The first two I never tried and running around, nobody ever asks me." Ann giggled and puffed at her cigarette. She was a beautiful girl, Mrs. Cannon told herself, and as nice as she was pretty. Some real gorgeous women, they acted like they owned the world and everybody else was dirt, but Ann Alspach wasn't that way. She acted like anybody else and she should be a Vegas showgirl with that face and that figure—gee, if that wolf Oliver could see her now in just her bra and panties, or when she had gotten out of the shower earlier that evening, his eyes would pop right out of his head and his tongue would hang out so far he could step on it.

She asked Ann if she was in show business, and the girl had said goodness no, she wasn't talented or anything, couldn't even carry a tune.

"Well, fashion modeling, then," Mrs. Cannon suggested "With your figure, you ought to be a big-time fashion model."

It developed that Ann had tried high-fashion modeling but she wasn't built for it, too much bust and hips for the Eastern fashion photographers. In California the Models had to be straight up and down, flat, with big feet, high cheekbones, and a sophisticated look.

"I know, I know," Mrs. Cannon sympathized. "My gawd, you look at some of those ads and you wonder if the girl is going to make it to the next blood transfusion."

"That's marvelous," Ann Alspach gurgled. "Honestly, you say the funniest things."

This endeared her to Mrs. Cannon's heart. At home, Joe used to be always saying for gawd' s sake, cut the corny comedy, either that or he wouldn't get the point, and Mrs. Cannon loved an audience. If she dared, she would have given Ann her imitations of Gracie Allan (poor Gracie) and Lucille Ball, but maybe that was too much of a good thing on what, after all, was short act.

"Well, what do you do then, honey?" she asked Ann, and the girl told her that she was a Computer-operator, whatever that was, something that Ann had had to take special training for, so it must be better than a typist's job.

"And I do some modeling," Ann confessed hesitantly. "Not fashion modeling, though. Its—sometimes I get a call to model for a life class San Francisco University." Mrs. Cannon nearly gasped out loud. "Do you mean bare, nude?" she asked. She had not meant to sound as shocked as it came out; what the hell, this was 1991 and some of the swimsuits they wore at the beach weren't much more than nothing at all, were they?

Ann Alspach nodded and rushed to her own defense. "It's not what most people think, Mrs. Cannon. A model in a life class, she's no more than something they can paint, no more than a still life or a landscape, honestly."

"You mean they don't get fresh, those artists?" Mrs. Cannon asked.

Ann shook her head firmly. "I never heard of a painter saying a wrong word to a model," she said. "They're —they're nutty, some of them, but they're not you-know. I mean, I'd rather pose in the nude for fifty art students than take a rush-hour BART subway ride from San Francisco, to

Oakland as far as getting poked and pinched and you—know—rubbed against and talked to, I mean." Mrs. Cannon looked at the wedding ring that had raised so many questions in the mind of George Oliver and asked, "What does your husband think about you posing in the altogether?"

"My husband?" Ann looked down at her left hand, and her face saddened before she made a pathetic attempt to smile. "That's all over," she explained. "Vance and I split up a long time ago, nearly two years."

"Oh," Mrs. Cannon said. "That's too bad."

"Yes, it was. But Vance was too brainy. It was all right for a while—Just wonderful—and then we found out we didn't have anything to talk about and you just can't keep on—well, I bored him. We never should have gotten married, I guess. It was a mistake."

"Yeah, he must have been brainy, like a moron," Mrs. Cannon snorted. "Anybody lets a girl like you get away must be off in the head."

"No, he—he felt as bad about it as I did, Mrs. Cannon. We parted friends and I—well, I still wear the ring sometimes to give me an excuse to say no, thanks, to fellows. It doesn't work often but it helps sometimes."

"You mean there's no boyfriend since this Vance played stupid and let you get away?"

"Vance isn't stupid," Ann protested. "I was the stupid one and that's why—well, about a boyfriend, I don't know whether you could call him that or not, but there's a man I like a lot. He's a painter, and someday he's going to be the greatest painter in the world."

"So what's he waiting for to make that wedding ring for real?"

Another shadow passed over the girl's beautiful face, and again Ann mustered a brave smile. "He says we can't get married till he gets somewhere with his art," she explained. "He knows—and I know, too— that he's going to be great someday but—well, it takes time for them to

110

realize how great you are. It takes years, sometimes. But I can wait. After Vance, I don't want him to make a mistake, like Vance did. I want him to be sure."

"What's his name?" Mrs. Cannon asked.

"Maybe I've seen some of his pictures."

Ann shook her head. "You may have but—well, he's pretty far out, Mrs. Cannon. His name's Pepper, the same as old Mr. Pepper on the jury. Dave Pepper." Now, as Mrs. Cannon watched her young roommate puff at her cigarette, she told herself that this Dave Pepper was a fool to hold off marrying this wonderful kid who had had it so bad with that dope Vance. Pepper either should get a regular job or start painting things that everybody would buy, like Norman Rockwell. Anything this beautiful wasn't going to wait around forever nor should she: she ought to get some nice man with a pile of money so he could give her everything she wanted. It would be worth it to him, Mrs. Cannon bet. That Vance couldn't talk to her; so with a wife like that, who needed to talk?

Ann should get somebody like Vitto 'Falconetti, only her own age and with a little more heat to him than that cold fish. Yes, 'Falconetti was handsome and he had half the money in the world and a first mortgage on the other half, but living with him, being his wife, couldn't be much fun. That Mrs. 'Falconetti sitting in the back of the courtroom didn't look as though she had gotten many laughs out of living with Vitto 'Falconetti, even if the clothes she had on must have come from Paris and the fur coat was worth a king's ransom, as the saying went.

Of coarse when a women's husband went on trial for hiring somebody to murder his business competitor, Mrs. Cannon supposed, she shouldn't look too happy. The way 'Falconetti acted during the trial, too; that couldn't have helped his wife's nerves much. No matter what the D.A. or the witnesses on that business deal said, 'Falconetti always looked as though he thought this was a lot of nonsense and he wanted to get it over with so he could go out and make a couple more million dollars.

So, she told herself, maybe that was the real proof that he was innocent. But how had that man Jaffee picked him out of all the people in California to make up that story about? And most of all, why didn't 'Falconetti get up there on the witness stand himself? Yeah, Mrs. Cannon knew it was his Constitutional right not to, but she, Vida Butts Cannon, sure would insist on it if she was in the same fix, God forbid.

CHAPTER THIRTEEN

"I'm putting you on the stand this afternoon," Rita Troyer told 'Falconetti, as the State neared the end of its presentation of witnesses.

'Falconetti turned his head slowly, his cat's-eye graygreen eyes showing their first faint indication of surprise. And concern? "What for?" he asked Rita.

"I think it'll help you," Troyer explained. "Things are going pretty welt but not quite well enough to make me comfortable. The prosecution scored some strong points with those details of the little under-the-counter deals you had going, ostensibly aimed at putting Dan Ferris out of business."

'Falconetti's shoulders moved under the exquisitely tailored cloth of his jacket. "I told you about that. Dan was getting ideas that he could be bigger than roe if he cut some comers, like on the Quigicy Building deal. He needed a little disciplining, that's all. I had to remind him how easy it would be to put him down if I wanted to get really rough on him,"

Rita nodded. "I know, but it would make a good impression on the jury if you explained it to them. Then, of course, there's still Jaffee's story."

'Falconetti snorted. "What about Jaffee? You made a bum out of him and he's all they have, really."

"I'm not so sure I demolished Jaffee quite that completely," Troyer said slowly. "I want you to get up there and make it positive. Ill ask you only one important question about Jaffee."

"Which is what?"

"Did you contract to have Daniel Ferriss murdered?

The big man shifted in his chair an uncharacteristic sign of uneasiness. "Why do you need that?" he asked.

"Anybody in his right mind would know I'd answer no if you asked me that. What good would it do me?"

"The jury wants to hear you say it," Troyer explained simply.

"All right, suppose I say it." 'Falconetti's tone roughened. "Then the D.A. will get up and make hash out of me."

Rita's eyebrows rose. "Can he?"

"What do you mean, can he?" 'Falconetti asked, then scowled. "Ah, come on. Counselor; we're not going to start that again, are we? No, I didn't do it."

Gary put, "it'll help a lot if you say so on the stand."

'Falconetti threw the PI the glance he usually gave him when he interjected a remark, one of thinly disguised annoyance. "You think so, Shamus?" he asked acidly. "I smile at the jury and fix everything and that gives the District Attorney his chance to do to me what your Boss did to Jaffee. I don't know whether I got through to you two at the time, but I told you that I've done things in my life that would curl that jury's hair if the D.A. got a chance to lay it all out in front of those people."

Arlaud had long since made himself ignore 'Falconetti's attitude toward him; it had not been easy, but the PI had built a philosophical defense against resentment toward clients who, consciously or not, were inclined to treat him as an office boy on occasion. Sooner or later most of them learned that Gary Arlaud carried his weight, and more, in the firm of Troyer Law Offices and those who didn't or wouldn't find this out were not important so long as Rita Troyer knew it and, more importantly, Gary Arlaud knew it.

"We haven't too much time," Rita Troyer said aloud. "How about it?"

Vitto 'Falconetti shook his head decisively. "I'm not going on that stand, Troyer."

"Even when I say I think it's important that you do?"

"No. Regardless of what you think. I'm not going to take the stand."

"Could you tell me why?" Rita asked curiously.

'Falconetti's eyes met hers squarely and his voice was matter-of-fact. "Suppose I said it was because I was afraid?"

Gary's surprise showed in his exclaim half-cry. "You, afraid? Afraid of what?"

"Of getting up there," 'Falconetti said heavily.

Rita made a slight gesture. "Well, naturally, everybody's a bit nervous about it, but let me assure you—"

'Falconetti cut her off, his voice savage. "What do you think I am, a pansy, Troyer? Nervous? I never drew a nervous breath in my life. I said I'd be afraid. I mean so I wouldn't be able to breathe. I mean so I wouldn't even know where I was or what I was saying. Do you understand me?"

Rita Troyer said gravely, "Mr. 'Falconetti, we're talking about your life. I'm not exaggerating when I say taking the stand or refusing lo may mean the difference between life and death for you."

The brickwork king shook his head again. "I don't care what it means," he said. "I'm not going to get up in. court in front of all those people and talk. Why? Because I can't." He held out his big hands. "Here, look at that," he said, and both Rita and Gary pinned their eyes on them, shocked by the violence of their tremors.

"I can't do it, that's all," 'Falconetti said, still quietly, still savagely. "If I do, I'll look guilty. They'll think I did it. They wouldn't understand it's something like— hell, call it stage fright. If I got up there- and shook for em, they'd forget all you've done to show up Jaffee as a lying bastard and the D.A. as a creep who's trying to prove that because I put an elbow into Ferriss' ribs with a couple of business deals, reminding him what was what, I had to hire a punk like Jaffee to kill him." His head wagged slowly back and forth. "No dice," he said. "Let's drop it. You've got this case locked up without calling me as a witness, so what's this all about?"

"No," Rita said soberly. "No, I haven't got this case locked up. I need you to do that."

"And I say I can't," Vitto 'Falconetti said tonelessly. "If staying off that witness stand means I get a bum verdict, then I get a bum verdict, that's all. I'm not getting on that stand Period."

CHAPTER FOURTEEN

Rita and Gary were at the Sonoma County Jail early the next morning to tell Vitto 'Falconetti about Charles Wolfe's not-too-veiled suggestion that the State would be willing to have him. plead guilty to second-degree murder or possibly even manslaughter, not only if the jury finally proved deadlocked but even while the jury deliberated.

The prisoner's face was gaunt with strain, his eyes were shadowed, for the first time since they had met him; it was evident that the night just passed had been an aching vigil for even tough-souled Vitto 'Falconetti.

"Let me get this straight," he asked, when Rita had finished outlining the situation. "Do you mean I can plead guilty to something that won't get me the Gas Chamber, even while that jerky jury is trying to make up their minds?"

"There's nothing guaranteed," Rita was careful to explain. "The District Attorney merely said he thought his office would entertain a lesser plea to save the time and expense of another trial in case of a hung jury. As for pleading to the lesser charge while the jury is out, it has been done. If I know the feelings of Mr. Wolfe and Judge Cleveland in this case, this might very well be one of the occasions on which the court would permit a last-minute—last-second, really—change of plea with the jury still out."

"You mean they're that mixed up about me?" 'Falconetti asked sardonically.

"Put simply, I guess that's about it," Troyer admitted.

'Falconetti murmured, "I'll be damned. When it's all so easy to figure, really. either I did or I didn't and you proved I didn't."

"I'm afraid I came a long way from proving you didn't, Mr. 'Falconetti," Rita said seriously. "If you'd taken the stand—but that's over and done with."

"Uh-huh," 'Falconetti said absently, then peered at Rita. "I'm paying you one hundred twenty-five thousand bucks for your good advice, so what's your advice now, Counselor?" he asked.

Rita said, "I'm sorry, but that's a decision you'll have to make yourself. I can only tell you that the jury was out several hours yesterday and didn't reach a verdict, proof enough that this is no open-and-shut acquittal. If the jury deadlocks and there's another trial, you may see fit to take the stand and give us the testimony that might have gotten that quick acquittal. On the other hand, say what you will, the defendant who stands trial a second time by reason of a hung jury bears the onus, acknowledged or subconscious, of the fact that the previous jury could not agree on his innocence. Most of all, you're the one who has to search your own soul. It's your life at stake, and nobody else has the right to tell you how to risk it or preserve it."

'Falconetti looked steadily at the lawyer and then said, Louise Parsons 'Falconetti was in the counsel room adjoining the courtroom half an hour before the court was scheduled to convene. Wolfe, knowing the deal was to be discussed, had agreed to the meeting between Vitto and Louise; the judge, for the same reason, had granted permission. When her husband was brought in, she left her chair and half-ran across the room to embrace him, holding him tight, her head against his chest, murmuring endearing incoherencies. Towering above her, his hands at his sides, Vitto 'Falconetti appeared neither embarrassed, touched, nor annoyed by this display. He looked over Lou's head at Rita, standing with Gary at the table beyond, and said in a level voice, "Okay, Troyer, suppose you lay it out for Mrs. 'Falconetti the same as you did for me this morning and see what she says." The woman drew back and looked up at her husband. Her face, so lovely, so carefully tended in her previous appearances in court, showed the ravages wrought by the night just passed. Her eyes were puffy, there were deep lines about her mouth; she seemed at least ten years older than her husband.

"Lay what out, Vitto?" she asked, her voice uncertain. "What's happened?"

Somehow 'Falconetti disengaged himself from her grasp without appearing to have raised a hand and walked toward the counsel table, talking back over his shoulder at his wife. "Troyer has come up with a great idea," he explained tonelessly. "She and the Shamus have got the jumps about what that jury is going to do, finally, so they've arranged an out for me. It seems that all of a sudden I have a choice."

"We didn't actually arrange an out for your husband, Mrs. 'Falconetti," Rita said. "Here, have a chair and I'll explain."

She watched as Louise made her way to the chair she drew out from the table, and as she approached, Rita was struck by the strange impression that Mrs. 'Falconetti was gripped by a fear quite separate from her dread that her husband would be found guilty and executed. Rita claimed no great intuitive powers for herself, but the impression she got so strongly was that Lou. 'Falconetti was burdened by a fear for herself, and she showed this by the haunted look she gave her big, handsome, wealthy husband as she passed him.

Now what? Rita asked herself dismally. 'Falconetti's no wife-hater, certainly, and even if he were, she's taken no part in the trial he might resent. Besides, isn't he leaving this vital decision up to her? And why is he doing this except out of his love and trust of her?

She turned these questions over in her mind, then discarded them as too complicated to be dealt with now, with the minutes ticking away. She took a seat across the table from the woman and briefly outlined the possibilities of the court and the prosecution entertaining a plea of guilty to a lesser charge.

She seemed dazed by this turn of events, shaken by the word that there could be a third outcome of the trial. She looked at Vitto and stammered, "Does Ms. Troyer mean that—that you—that it doesn't make any difference what the jury—"

"Hell, she spelled it all out for you, Lou," 'Falconetti interrupted. "Either I take my chances with the jury or I go in and tell them I did it, I'm sorry, send me off to the pen. If I decide to tough it out and the jury says not guilty, it's all a mistake, why, then I can come home to you and take up where I left off, all the unfinished business."

Rita Troyer asked herself whether her imagination was playing tricks on her or did that last carry an ominous undertone).

"But—but that's your decision, Vitto, not mine," Lou said after a long pause.

"And I'm turning it over to you," 'Falconetti said.

The woman turned toward Rita. "Tell him he has to decide, Ms. Troyer."

The lawyer shook her head. "He's made it clear that the decision's up to you, Mrs. 'Falconetti," she said quietly, sympathetically.

Lou turned back to Vitto. "But why?" she asked. "Why make me decide?"

The sardonic voice was gone, and for the first time in the Rita's hearing, 'Falconetti spoke softly, gently. "Because you've got as much at stake as me, Lou, maybe more. You've always known the score. You know it now."

"But you've never left anything important up to me to decide," she complained, almost petulantly.

"I was never up against exactly the same problem," 'Falconetti retorted. "Before, what concerned me, I took care of, and what was your business, you handled. No sweat. But this thing has got both of us mixed in it right up to here. Dan was your friend as well as mine. I don't know, maybe you wonder if maybe I didn't have him knocked off over the Quigley deal or because—"

"No, Vitto," she said. "No. Of course not."

"Well, there are all these angles," 'Falconetti said. "I been figuring angles all my life, but now there are Just too many for me so I want you to take over and say the word."

"Angles?" she asked.

"A million angles. I thought we had this case won, hands down; now I find out we don't, not by a long shot. I never figured there'd be any question that I'd walk out of here as free as a goddam bird, but now it seems there's one hell of a big question. So how do you say we play it, Lou? Do I cop a plea and maybe get sent away for maybe ten-to-twenty years? Or do I stick with the jury and maybe get an acquittal so I can come home with you?" His mouth twisted as he said, "It's been a million years since we've been together without a crowd around us, Lou. There'll be plenty to talk over, hub?"

Again Rita saw (or thought she saw) a passing shadow of fear.

"Why, yes," Louise said. "Of course. I don't know what to say. Or rather— well, this is what I think, Vitto. Either you committed this—this thing or you didn't. If you didn't, why should you plead guilty to anything? If you k-k-killed Dan—oh, Vitto, I know you didn't, you didn't!" She stopped, her head dropping.

"Go ahead, Lou," he said steadily. "If I killed him, what?"

She raised her head with an effort, and Rita could see the tears glistening in her eyes. "If you did, I don't see how the law could let you lie and say it was something besides c-cold-blooded murder."

'Falconetti said, "Well, they don't exactly claim I killed Dan cold-bloodedly, whatever that's supposed to mean. According to Dick Wolfe in there, I'm supposed to have given that creep Jaffee a thousand bucks to do it for me."

"That would be worse," she choked. "A thousand times worse. But you didn't do it! You didn't!"

"So?" 'Falconetti asked.

She struggled to find words. "I don't know. I always thought that all you, or anybody else, was entitled to was a fair trial. I suppose you got that, didn't you, Vitto?"

"Mrs. 'Falconetti," Rita put in, "there are times when expediency makes sense. Right now it could be the difference between your husband's living and dying."

"But will it be?" Louise asked desperately. "Do you know what that jury's going to do?"

"No," Troyer admitted.

"And if Vitto lives because of your expediency, where and how will he live?"

"In prison."

"Like—like a man, a human being?"

"As close as they can come to it," Rita said.

The woman looked down at her hands, twisting in her lap. "You don't offer much, do you?" she asked, after a long pause.

"Now, Lou," 'Falconetti said, "what do you mean by that? If I was put away I could work hard and keep my nose clean, and before you knew it I'd be coming home with a parole in my hand and it would be like it was before. Or almost, anyway. I'd be a little older and you'd be a little older, but you know me, Lou; I'd be the same man, I wouldn't change. Other people forget things or change their mind or decide half-finished is good enough, but not Vitto 'Falconetti."

Rita saw Mrs. 'Falconetti wince as though lashed, and something, the beginning of a thought, ail idea, an explanation, stirred in the back of his mind. "Well, Lou?" 'Falconetti asked. "We haven't got all day." Louise kept her eyes on her hands, and her lips barely moved as she said, "I say no deal."

Rita saw the beginnings of a humorless grin curl one corner of 'Falconetti's mouth as the big man turned toward her. "Give the little lady a great big hand, Troyer," he said, his voice back to its cold, toneless level. "You'd better tell the D.A. that on advice of my dearly beloved wife, who's been married to me all these years with never a cross word between us, I've decided to take my chances with the jury. And if Lori guessed wrong— well, she always did look good in black."

Ignoring the shredded cry that broke from his wife's knuckled lips, he said briskly, "And now I guess we'd better get into that courtroom, eh, and wait for the news." And added, almost negligently, "You'd better stay here, Lou. Anything I hate it's one of those soap operas when the man gets up and says it's too bad but the defendant has thrown an acey-deucy, F--k him."

****

The word from the jury room was a long time in coming, or at least it seemed a long time to Rita and Gary, Charley Wolfe, Louise Parsons 'Falconetti and, presumably, the man whose life was at stake, Vitto 'Falconetti.

The morning hours crawled by without word from the jury, not even the request for a piece of the evidence transcript. 'Falconetti played gin rummy with Gary in the counsel room, building his score with gins, canny high go-downs, and undercuts. At her husband's urging, Louise 'Falconetti kept a hair appointment, leaving only after Gary promised to call Karle's the moment any word developed so that she could hurry back to the courtroom.

"But no plastic curlers in your hair," 'Falconetti warned her as he took her kiss on the comer of his mouth.

Rita tried to imagine Louise 'Falconetti with pink plastic curlers in her hair, wearing a babushka, and couldn't. But then, she told herself, she couldn't imagine a wife keeping a hair appointment while the jury was out deciding her husband's fate, either. She asked herself why Louise was afraid, why she had winced at her husband's reminder that he did not forget things. Why did 'Falconetti bear down so hard on his promise to come out of prison with a parole (if that was what Louise decided), ready and able to take up where he had left off?

That remark, Other people decide half-finished is good enough but not Vitto 'Falconetti, what did that mean?

Half-finished. Had 'Falconetti meant that he wasn't finished, and did Louise 'Falconetti fear what he might do to her when this was all over, if he was acquitted? And did that mean that Ferriss had been one half, that she would be the second half? Had she and Ferriss been lovers? If so, that would mean that 'Falconetti had had Ferriss killed, not for business reasons but out of revenge.

Rita shook her head. Too late for such thoughts now. If the jury was hung and there was a second trial, perhaps she could explore these possibilities and, if they proved out, base a defense on the premise of a cuckolded husband avenging a great wrong. If such a thing had happened and if 'Falconetti would tell her the story—but there was little likelihood of 'Falconetti admitting such a thing even if it were true.

Which it wasn't. Of course it wasn't.

She left the room shortly after Mrs. 'Falconetti had departed and made her way to the empty courtroom to go over some notes concerning another case. She was studying her own hieroglyphics, trying to decipher the scribble that only Rory, her secretary, seemed able to untangle, when Charles Wolfe entered the room, went to the prosecution table, looked over at Rita, and then crossed to the defense attorney. "Your boy hasn't changed his mind, has he, Rita?" he asked gloomily.

"No, be hasn't," Troyer said, and tossed the folder on the table in front of her. She leaned back in her chair, smiling. She liked Charley. The Assistant D.A. had one of the best over-all scores against the Troyer Law Firm of the whole District Attorney's staff, but each of Wolfe's wins had been hard-fought, along the strict line of law, with no razzel dazzel, no more vindictiveness, at least, no more than was demanded of a public prosecutor who believed he had a guilty man to bring to justice.

"Have you heard anything?" Rita asked.

"Not a thing," Charley replied.

"You?"

"No, and I'd give a day's pay to hear what they're talking about."

"You couldn't afford it," Wolfe said. He looked toward the door that led to the jury room. "They ought to be going out to lunch pretty soon."

"What do you think, Charley?" Rita asked. "Just between us girls."

"I think they'll each eat six and a half dollars' worth, right on the button, and complain about the food all the way back here."

"No, seriously," Troyer said.

"You're asking me, Rita? About a jury? I'm betting they finally admit they're hung, but I haven't won a bet since the Lehigh-Lafayetfe game of

1981." Rita sighed. "I'd give a whole year's income not to have to start from scratch again on this case, Charley. And that I really can't afford."

Wolfe shoved his hands deep in his pockets and scowled at the table. "I'd hate to see 'Falconetti get off, Rita," he said in a low voice. "I guess that's why I was hoping he'd take us up on that pica offer. There's always the chance that jury may—and he is guilty, Rita Guilty for sure."

Rita pursed her lips and then shook her head faintly. "I don't think he is," she said after a pause. "I know he's capable of it, but I don't think he did it. Not this one."

Wolfe hesitated, then blurted. "He did this one, too, Rita, believe me. I suppose I shouldn't be telling you this, but I had another line to base my case on. I had a choice of two ways to go, and I picked this one as the stronger. But now I don't know. I really don't know." And the second line was that 'Falconetti had Ferriss killed because he was Mrs. 'Falconetti's lover? The question trembled on Troyer's lips, but it died there. "Well," he said with an attempt at joviality, "if you win the first bet since 1981 and the jury's hung, you may have your chance to try the other line, Charley."

"God forbid," Wolfe said piously.

"Amen," Troyer echoed.

At 2:47 P.M. the jury gave the word to Ed Hammersma, the court officer, that it had reached a verdict and was ready to report it out. The news streaked to the room where Troyer and 'Falconetti were waiting. Gary reached for the telephone to call Mrs. 'Falconetti or at least to call Karie's salon to see if she had left a forwarding number if she was not there, but 'Falconetti cut him short with a gesture.

'"Don't call," he ordered Gary. "It will be better without her here, either way it goes."

Gary started to protest, subsided at his boss's headshake. The trio started for the door. Midway across the room, 'Falconetti paused and reached

124

into an inside coat pocket to bring out a small piece of paper, tightly folded. He gave this to Rita, explaining, "Here you are, Troyer. Read it after they give the verdict and I'm gone, either back to the can or wherever they take a guy that's acquitted."

"What is it?" Troyer asked.

"Never mind; you'll see. I just figured—maybe I figured I owed you this. You worked hard. You earned your one hundred twenty-five grand, all right. I couldn't sleep very well last night, and so when. I woke up about five I got the turnkey to get me a pencil and some paper and I wrote it down for you." His mouth crooked and he said, "Please excuse the mistakes. I have a high-priced secretary to clean up my English and do my spelling for me, you know. But it's all down there. It's all privileged, too, isn't it? I mean, no matter how you might hate my guts, you wouldn't cross me because I leveled with you, would you?"

Rita shook her head. "No," she said, "but I claim the right to use anything you may have written to influence my decision about representing you if there's another trial."

"There won't be, not about Dan, anyway," 'Falconetti said. "This is either fly away, yellow bird, or Katie bar the door."

"But the appeals in case—"

"I'll take my chances that you'll feel obligated to go along with me if we need to appeal," 'Falconetti interrupted. 'That's one thing about you, Troyer; you've got integrity coming out your ears. If the word's bad, you could no more cut me loose than you could fly—you'd think you hadn't done the honorable thing by running out on a guy when he was down, or some such horse manure."

Before Rita could speak, 'Falconetti said sharply, "So let's go. You were the one that said the judge was nobody to keep waiting, remember?"

Rita, Vitto, Gary and the court officer walked down the corridor to the court room, and the defendant and his attorney tool; their places at the defense table. Rita exchanged one glance with Charley Wolfe and knew by the D.A.'s expression that no word of the jury's verdict had been leaked to him. The jury filed into the box, Anson Benedict and Charles Williams, Mrs. Vida Cannon and Ann Alspach, John Crier and Louis Kobe], Elsie Harding and Mrs. Lorraine Brown, Harry Stetler and Old Man Pepper, and, finally, George Oliver and the foreman, Walton Robinson.

"What do you think?" 'Falconetti asked Rita Troyer in an undertone.

"I don't know. Their faces are always the same, blank. I've been told so many times about juries—if they look at the defendant, they say, he's acquitted; if they don't he's convicted. It doesn't mean a thing. Half of them are looking at you and the other half aren't. Take your pick."

Hammersma, standing beside the door to the judge's chambers, got his signal, opened the door, and slapped his hand against the wood-paneled wall twice, barking, "All rise."

'Falconetti got to his feet, flanked by Rita, as the spectators clattered and coughed behind them. They stood there while Judge Harrison Cleveland mounted the bench and sat down; then they took their seats again. The Judge nodded to the clerk, and the cleric turned to ask Walton Robinson, "Mr. Foreman, have you reached a verdict?"

"We have," Robinson said.

"Will the foreman face the defendant?" the clerk asked, and turned toward the defense table. "Will the defendant rise and face the Jury?"

"Here we go," 'Falconetti breathed as he got to his feet, accompanied by Rita.

"What is your verdict?" the clerk asked the jury foreman.

Walton Robinson's voice caught in his throat. He coughed to clear it, then spoke shrilly. "We the jury in the above entitled action do find the defendant not guilty."

Rita Troyer heard the exhalation of a long sigh from the man beside her. The lawyer wanted to savor her own relief, the relief born of the knowledge that there would be no retrial, no need for appeals, but the buoyancy failed to come. Instead, there was that folded sheet of paper in her attaché case, telling her what she almost knew now.

"Ladies and gentlemen of the jury," the clerk was reciting, "hearken to your verdict. You say you find the defendant, Vitto 'Falconetti, not guilty of the crime charged in the indictment, and so say you all. Is that your verdict?" After the foreman's affirmative answer, the jury was polled, on Wolfe's motion. One by one, each of the jurors answered, "Yes, that's my verdict."

Judge Cleveland's voice was entirely noncommittal. "The Jury is dismissed with the thanks of the court," he said. "Since you have sat in a capital case, I will order that any of you who wish to be excused from further jury duty, permanently and for all time, need only to advise the clerk and you will be so excused. The defendant is released from custody herewith. Court is adjourned."

When the judge had left the bench to go through the side door, his robe billowing behind him, 'Falconetti turned to Rita Troyer. Gone was all trace of haggardness or shadowed eyes; the big man was the same superior, untouchable figure he had been the first time Troyer had laid eyes on him.

"Maybe I ought to tell you to give me that letter back, Troyer," he said, "but I won't, don't ask me why. Maybe I want you to have it just in case anything happens." He gave a short laugh. "Or maybe I just want to bug you— you and all the other fine, upstanding women of honor." He started to leave, then turned back and said, "Oh, and thanks, Troyer. You did real good." He looked at Gary and added grudgingly, "Both of you did." Rita nodded without speaking. Gary murmured something and then said, "I'll send you my check for The Gin game

The big man shook his head, reached into his pocket. "I said double or nothing if I was acquitted, didn't I? Call it."

"Heads," Gary said as the coin flickered in the air. 'Falconetti cupped his palm over the coin as it landed on the back of his other hand. He lifted the top hand and peered, then grinned at Gary Arlaud. "Good call," he said. "First time you've been right at this game."

He said, "Be seeing you, maybe," and turned and walked toward the nearest door, straight, tall, wide shouldered, superbly self-assured, contemptuous of the men about him and of any and all events that might try to stop Vitto: 'Falconetti from doing what he wanted to do.

The unsigned note was full of misspellings and the handwriting was wretched, but it told Rita Troyer what she wanted to know and what she had suspected, at the very end.

First off (it said) I know this punk Jaffee from way back. He even did some jobs for me. None of them important but enough I know he is a small time crook on the side.

And this spook has the nerve to try to shake me down with some pictures he took of my best friend and the only woman I ever loved. You can't figure it. They probably was careful as hell nobody saw them and when they get there they never think to pull down the shades. Jaffee is laying brick on an apartment house across the street and he knows who they are. When this keeps up he steals a good camera and brings it along on the job in lunch pail and finally he gels three or four pictures you cant help but recknize them both. He came to me I dont know why instead of Ferriss or Lou and I tell him sure he'll get his thousand bucks he wants but I don't have it on me only a couple hundred. I gave him two bills for the pictures and films

128

and I said Id meet him the next Day at a certain corner at a certain time with the other eight hundred. He believes me and I call Dan and tell him this guy he phoned me about having some pictures of he and Lou. I say I dont believe it but he better fix this guy or he will spread it all around. I tell him to find this guy Jaffee at a certain corner and fix him good. He better do it personnal not one of h!s boys and he says all right because he knows I'll kill him if I he leive Jaffee, him and Lou, both. So I foned Jaffee at the number he gave me and I said Ferriss found out and he wants to pay five thousand for the pictures. I said Id like to see him screwwed before I kill him so meet Ferriss at the corner instead of me and get some dough out of him by saving he'll give him the pictures. I know Jaffee is a stupid jerk and like I though! he believes me. I said he better take a gun in caw Ferris gets rough. He said he dont have a gun and I arranged for him to get one and never mind how.

It worked like I knew it would because Dan Ferriss never would stand still long when a punk like Jaffee tried to squeeze him. Only thing I don't know who is going to kill who but either way it was all right. If Dan kills Jaffee I tip them off about it and I would even testify against him because he gave me the best friend manure ail along. If you think Jaffee lied on the stand you didnt hear nothing side of what Id say lo make sure Dan Ferriss got it good.

I dont know how Jaffee got the nerve to kill Dan but he did and thats the main thing. Now if the jury votes guilty it dont make much differance except I would like lo take care of some unfinish business before I crap out.

Dan Ferris was one of only two people that were in the pictures and I never left anybody get away with anything like that for long.

Rita Troyer folded the note and put it in her pocket. How privileged was a thing like this when the case was over and if, by acting upon it, a woman might be protected from—what? Being murdered? Hardly: Vitto 'Falconetti must have a more exquisite torture planned for the wife who had betrayed him. How could she, Rita Troyer, act without being guilty of a breach of trust, and if she did intervene) what difference could she make in the eventual outcome?

And Louise 'Falconetti, had she voted against her husband's pleading to a lesser charge because she secretly hoped the jury would vote guilty and so let the Gas Chamber free her of the menace of her husband's revenge? Or did she love him despite her affair with Ferriss and prefer whatever punishment he might plan for her to life without him, the dreary years that would stretch out while Vitto served out his prison sentence, earned for the killing of her paramour?

She started, looked up, as Charley Wolfe spoke her name. The Assistant District Attorney had his hand thrust out and a brave attempt at a smile on his round face. "Congratulations, Rita," he said.

Rita stood up and accepted his hand. "Thanks, Charley," she managed.

Wolfe's eyes moved from Rita to Gary, and then he forced a wry laugh. "Believe it or not, Rita, it helps, knowing I was right. I can guess what was in that letter." His eyes took on a mocking glint that Rita had never before seen there, but he said nothing.

"Well, Rita," the Assistant D.A. said, "there you go. Do you want me to pin the tag on you now?"

"What tag?" Troyer asked warily.

"The one that says KICK ME HARD."

Rita flushed, then lost her anger as quickly as it had claimed! her. "You know better than that, Charley," she said.

He looked toward the jury box, where the eight men and four women were still saying their good-bys, George Oliver trying to move in on Ann Alspach.

"It was their decision," Rita said, "not mine."

Wolfe nodded. "And God protect us from them. Since when have they ever known what they were doing?"

"Charley, Charley," Rita said softly. "You know where we'd be without juries."

"Maybe we'd be better off."

"Hold it, Charley. You know how the law works just as well as I do. Once in a while a guilty man goes free, as 'Falconetti just did. We can afford that a hell of a lot better than we can afford to have an innocent man convicted. Better men than you or I arranged for that, Charley, and it works and you know it works."

There was a pause and finally Charley Wolfe nodded reluctantly. "Sure it works," he said. "I Just happen to be a bum loser, that's all."

"I don't know exactly who's the winner in this one," Troyer said quizzically.

"I sure don't feel like one. 'Falconetti's life was saved, but I don't think that's going to be any joyride from here on in. His wife—but the trial's over, that's the main thing. Let's the three of us go out and see if we can find a stray St. Bernard with a small keg around its neck, shall we?"

No-Lo

EPILOGUE

Two months after the 'Falconetti trial ended in acquittal, Gary was reading his Press Democrat at the breakfast bar, a cup of coffee in his hand, when he uttered an exclamation, put down his cup, and reached for the telephone.

"Rita?" he said, when there finally was an answer at the other end. "Have you read the PD yet? Yes, I know it's Sunday but . . .. well, listen; you'll want to hear this."

And he read, slowly, distinctly. "AP San Francisco, yesterday's date. Vitto H. 'Falconetti of—his address—long a prominent figure in the Bay Area building trades, and his wife, the former Louise Parsons of Baltimore, Maryland, were fatally injured late tonight when 'Falconetti's powerful sports car apparently went out of control on the Coast Highway South of the City near here went over a cliff and crashed in the ocean, and the rocks below.

"Witnesses estimated the small roadster was traveling at well over a hundred miles an hour when it suddenly careened crazily and sailed over to edge and the rocks below. Doctors at San Francisco General where the Couple were taken by helicopter Ambulance. They were pronounced DOA.

'Falconetti was acquitted of charges on having contracted for the murder of a business rival Danial Ferriss by a Santa Rosa Jury where the case was heard on a change of venue. . . . .

ABOUT THE AUTHOR

Steve Arleaux (Arlo) was born Gary Arlaud (Arlo) in 1944 at Des Moines Iowa and had his name legally changed due to a lifetime of bad pronunciations. Steve joined the navy in 1961. The highlight of his Navy time was going around the world on the USS Enterprise in 1964.

After returning to the United States from a law enforcement career (Caribbean Cops, II, III, IV VI see Amazon.Com) in St. Croix, the US Virgin Islands. He got into the oil business and again traveled the world as a Target Drilling Consultant for an International Corporation.

In 1989 while working for Drilco in the Geothermal fields in Northern California he was laid off along with 250,000 oil workers worldwide, he went back to his old trade and became a Private Investigator in Santa Rose California and worked on a contract basis for the local PD on weekends.

Eventually he migrated back to his hometown of Des Moines (See Caribbean Cops VII out next year).

Steve currently lives near the Gulf Coast in Mississippi and is enjoying the warm weather and his retirement. Steve keeps his hand in the business and does security work on a part time basis.

Steve holds a BS in Liberal Arts, with a minor in Philosophy from Iowa State University, he also holds a Masters in Political Science/International Relations with a specialty in "The Politics of Terrorism" and "International Political Economics" Steve has taught as an adjunct professor in these areas, and does consulting work for the international business community